Oliver Raymond

The Art of Fishing on the Principle of Avoiding Cruelty

With Approved Rules for Fishing, Used During Sixty Years' Practice....

Oliver Raymond

The Art of Fishing on the Principle of Avoiding Cruelty
With Approved Rules for Fishing, Used During Sixty Years' Practice....

ISBN/EAN: 9783337157678

Printed in Europe, USA, Canada, Australia, Japan

Cover: Foto ©Andreas Hilbeck / pixelio.de

More available books at **www.hansebooks.com**

THE ART
OF
FISHING

ON THE PRINCIPLE OF

AVOIDING CRUELTY.

WITH

APPROVED RULES FOR FISHING

USED DURING SIXTY YEARS' PRACTICE, NOT HITHERTO
PUBLISHED IN ANY WORK ON THE SUBJECT.

BY THE

REV. OLIVER RAYMOND, LL.B.

LONDON:
LONGMANS, GREEN, AND CO.
1866

DEDICATION.

TO

MY WORTHY AND EXCELLENT FRIEND

THE REV. JAMES MULES, LL.B.

A FRIENDSHIP of not less than sixty years, and that friendship uninterrupted, we have experienced through boyhood and manhood; companions in recreation and toil; the former more especially in our favourite amusement of "fishing," when in early life we passed our school-boy days, forgetful, I fear, that those hours were intended, not to teach the young idea how to fish, but how to shoot. Our recreation, let me believe, however, was not a vicious one,—for the good old Izaak Walton tells us that Angling is an art worthy the knowledge and practice of a wise man, and that contemplation and action belong to this honest, ingenuous, quiet, and harmless art of Angling.

It is with no small degree of pleasure I dedicate this treatise, on the best mode of rendering fishing a merciful pursuit, to you, my early friend, knowing that I place it in the hands of one possessed with the milk of human kindness, and who, mindful of that celebrated passage in Shakespeare,—"the poor beetle "which we tread upon finds a pang as great as when a "giant dies,"—would not wantonly and unnecessarily hurt the smallest insect. " Blessed are the merciful, " for they shall obtain mercy," is a voice from Heaven, to be heard, not in behalf of man alone, but of all God's creatures here on earth. Although an almost uninterrupted prosecution of the duties of our high calling have left you little time and leisure, in middle and later life, to follow the pursuit of which I have taken in hand to hold converse, yet I well know your taste and relish for fishing have never been lost; nor have you seen cause to condemn it, if followed in a way of wise moderation, and in subservience to those claims of duty which devolve upon every Christian, and, with accumulated force and sanction, on every Christian minister.

With every sentiment of regard, esteem, and friendship,

I subscribe myself,

My dear and valued friend,

Yours most faithfully,

THE AUTHOR.

PREFACE.

So MANY publications on the art of fishing have issued from the press, that it might appear at first sight superfluous to say anything further on the subject. The art, it is true, has been largely developed, still it appears to one accustomed to this fascinating amusement for more than sixty years, that some few fresh hints might be given to render it more complete. This, however, is not the principal object of this work, written, according to its title, to reduce the practice to the principle of mercy. We speak here as regards *comparative* mercy; since field and river sports cannot in themselves be devoid altogether of pain and suffering to those animals or fish we endeavour to capture. I would here, by the way, remark that the river sport is far less cruel than the field sports. This will be considered a bold remark; but I fear not to carry out its truth in the following treatise, and to show clearly (if my directions be followed) that the former sport is mercy compared with the latter.

Here are no broken legs or wings in half-shot hares and birds to torment the sufferers—no lengthened course to agonise the pursued till their hearts are broken—a frequent occurrence in the hunted hare. We might here allude also to the patient fox, pursued, run down, and torn limb from limb by its voracious enemies, yet never heard to complain. As well again to the timid hunted deer, whose piteous cries and tears " in " vain bespeak her grief." Death, it is true, is the fate of the captured fish, but not a *lingering* death, unless unnecessarily made so by the merciless fisherman. This I have to prove, and this is the object of the present little work—its *principal* object, though combined with some few hints on the art of fishing, which may not have appeared in former publications; for, in truth, unless from recollection, not one direction has been copied from any work on fishing: they are all original.

> "Better precepts if you can impart,
> "Why do: I'll follow them with all my heart,"

is the observation of Horace, as copied by a well-known writer on the art of angling. In this quotation, if applied to merciful rules in fishing, I gladly concur; it being a certain fact, the more mercy we show in our sports and pastimes, the more shall we enjoy the same, especially in those hours we spend in the noble art of angling.

The state of our fisheries, whether in the sea or our large rivers, as a supply of cheap and wholesome food for the teeming millions of our increasing population, has attracted attention in Parliament, and among thinking and benevolent persons. Should the subject attain its due weight and just proportion of interest, it will be no small service to the cause of human happiness and improvement that the principle of mercy in the capturing of fish should prevail.

During the pleasing hours occupied in compiling these sheets, a curious legendary tale fell in the author's way, which, although it exhibits a sample of the marvellous, painted in glowing colours by a heated fancy, yet, under the guise of fable, there are certain lessons of philosophy, amid much of exaggeration and paradox indeed, that we offer no apology for introducing it to the curious among our readers. The account is taken from the second volume of Addison's "Travels." That such a writer allowed it a place in his works, entitles this literary curiosity to a passing notice.

St. Anthony is also very famous for his sermons; the most remarkable of which is that which he preached to a company of fishes. As the audience and the sermon are both extraordinary, I shall set down the account at length. When the heretics would not regard his preaching, he betook himself to the sea-shore, where the river Marechia disembogues itself into the Adriatic. He called the fishes together in the name of God, that they might hear his Holy Word. The fish came swimming towards him in such vast shoals, both from the sea and from the river, that the surface of the water was quite covered with their multitudes. They quickly ranged themselves, according to their several species, into a very beautiful congregation, and like so many rational creatures presented themselves before him to hear the Word of God. St. Anthony was so struck with the miraculous obedience and submission of these poor animals, that he found a secret sweetness distilling upon his soul, and at last addressed himself to them in the following words:—

"Although the infinite power and providence of God, "my dearly beloved fishes, discovers itself in all the works "of His creation, as in the heavens, in the sun, and in the "moon, and in the stars—in this lower world, in man, "and in the other perfect creatures—nevertheless the "goodness of the Divine Majesty shines out in you "more eminently, and appears after a particular manner, "than in any other created beings. For notwithstand-"ing you are comprehended under the name of reptiles, "partaking of a middle nature between stones and "beasts, and imprisoned in the deep abyss of waters; "notwithstanding you are tossed among billows, thrown "up and down by tempests, deaf to hearing and dumb "to speaking, and terrible to behold; notwithstanding, "I say, these natural disadvantages, the Divine goodness "shows itself in you after a very wonderful manner. "In you are seen the mighty mysteries of an infinite "goodness. The Holy Scripture has always made use "of you as the types and shadows of some profound "sacrament. Do you think that without a mystery, "that the first present that God Almighty made to man "was of you, O ye fishes? Do you think that without "a mystery, among all creatures and animals which "were appointed for sacrifices, you only were excepted? "Do you think there was nothing meant by our "Saviour Christ, that next to the Paschal Lamb, he "took so much pleasure in the food of you, O ye fishes? "Do you think it was by mere chance, that when "the Redeemer of the world was to pay a tribute to

"Cæsar, he saw fit to find it in the mouth of a fish? "These are all of them so many mysteries and sacra- "ments, that oblige you in a more particular manner "to the praises of your Creator.

"It is from God, my beloved fish, that you have "received being, life, motion, and sense. It is He that "has given you a compliance with your natural incli- "nation, the whole world of waters for your habitation. "It is He that has furnished it with lodgings, chambers, "caverns, grottoes, and such magnificent retirements "as are not to be met with in the chambers of kings, "or in the palaces of princes. You have the water for "your dwelling—a clear, transparent element, brighter "than crystal. You can see from its deepest bottom "everything that passes on its surface. You have the "eyes of a lynx, or of an Argus. You are guided by a "secret unerring principle, delighting in everything "that may be beneficial to you, and avoiding every- "thing that may be hurtful. You are carried on by a "hidden instinct to preserve yourselves, and to propa- "gate your species. You obey, in all your actions, "works, and motions, the dictates and suggestions of "Nature, without the least repugnancy or contradiction. "The colds of winter and the heats of summer are "equally incapable of molesting you. A serene or "clouded sky are indifferent to you. Let the earth "abound in fruits or be cursed with scarcity, it has no "influence on your welfare. You live secure in rains "or thunders, lightnings and earthquakes. You have

"no concern in the blossoms of spring or in the glow-
"ings of summer, in the fruits of autumn or the frosts of
"winter. You are not solicitous about hours or days,
"or months or years, the variableness of the weather
"or the change of seasons. In what dreadful majesty,
"in what wonderful power, in what amazing providence
"did God Almighty distinguish you among all the
"species of creatures that perished in the universal
"Deluge! You only were insensible of the mischief
"that had laid waste the whole world. All this, as I
"have already told you, ought to inspire you with
"gratitude and praise towards the Divine Majesty that
"has done so great things for you, granted you such
"particular graces and privileges, and heaped upon you
"so many distinguished favours.

"And since for all this you cannot employ your
"tongues in the praises of your Benefactor, and are not
"provided with words to express your gratitude, make
"at least some sign of reverence, bow yourselves at His
"name. Give some show of gratitude according to the
"best of your capacities; express your thanks in the
"most becoming manner you are able; and be not
"unmindful of all the benefits He has bestowed on you."

He had no sooner done speaking than behold a miracle! The fish, as though they had been endued with reason, bowed their heads with all the marks of profound humility and devotion, moving their bodies up and down with a kind of fondness, as approving what had been spoken by St. Anthony.

The legend adds, that many heretics who were present at the miracle were converted by it; and that St. Anthony gave his benediction to the fish and dismissed them.

Although to the Christian's mind the trifling, not to say profane appeal to the sacred name be justly offensive and revolting, yet are there touches of feeling and sentiment underlying this fabulous invention worthy of notice—the wonders in the world of waters, whether in ocean, lake, or river, manifested in the variegated displays of the Creator's power and wisdom in the formation of the inhabitants thereof, in the provision made for their sustenance and well-being—as cannot but add weight to the leading argument of the ensuing work.

With peculiar satisfaction I close these prefatory remarks by directing the attention of my readers to an extract by the pen of the distinguished author of "Salmonia." Though I would not venture to endorse *every sentiment* made by all his characters, about some of which there may well be a difference of opinion, yet I take leave to transfer to my pages one exquisitely lovely and priceless gem of beauty, establishing the claims of our art for fostering contemplation on subjects of the deepest interest to humanity.

Physicus.—I envy no quality of the mind or intellect in others; not genius, power, wit, or fancy. But if I could choose what would be most delightful, and I believe most useful to me, I should prefer a firm religious belief to every other blessing : for it makes life a discipline of goodness, creates new hopes when all earthly hopes vanish, and throws over the decay, the destruction of existence, the most gorgeous of all lights, awakens life even in death, and from corruption and decay calls up beauty and divinity, makes an instrument of torture and of shame the ladder of ascent to paradise; and far above all combinations of earthly hopes, calls up the most delightful visions of palms and amaranths, the gardens of the blest, the security of everlasting joys, where the sensualist and the sceptic view only gloom, decay, annihilation, and despair.*

---

* *Salmonia*, p. 136. By the late Sir Humphry Davy.

AD LECTOREM.

Gentle Reader, if this name
Fits your character, no blame
Will you cast on this endeavour
Fishing sports from pain to sever.
Only follow out my book,
Then no wriggling worm on hook,
Nor live roach, nor gudgeon spitted,
Dying by inches and unpitied,
Nor captured fish, e'en death denied,
Gasping by the water-side,
Left in agony to pine,
Shall disgrace your rod and line.
" Mercy," so our poet sings,*
" Like the dew on earthly things,
" Falls from heaven, to embrace
" Man below with her sweet grace."
I will, then, entreat her well
While she deigns with me to dwell;
And for love will I escort her
In her search beneath the water.
On a sunbeam we will glide,
Sweet companions, side by side,
Where, amidst their oozy beds,
River weeds entwine their threads,
And joyful fishes shall in her see
Their longed-for benefactress, Mercy.
  My aim, then, do not judge absurd,
But come with us and make a third;
Fair Mercy first, then you and I,
With ground bait, minnow, net, or fly.

C. A. R.

* Shakespeare's *Merchant of Venice*.

CONTENTS.

CHAPTER I.

REMARKS ON NETS AND TACKLE TO BE USED IN FISHING, BUT PRINCIPALLY ON THE CASTING NET—HOW TO TAKE UP AND DELIVER . . . . *Page* 1

CHAPTER II.

OF THE "LANDING NET"—HOW IT SHOULD BE MADE AND HOW CARRIED 10

CHAPTER III.

OF THE "HOOP OR BOW NET"—ITS SIZE—HOW TO SET AND HOW TO BAIT IT 13

CHAPTER IV.

CONTAINS SEVERAL PARTICULARS RELATING TO THE "FLEW NET"—ITS SIZE—DESCRIBING THE LINT AND WALL—HOW TO SET 16

CHAPTER V.

UPON THE CHOICE OF YOUR ANGLE ROD, WHETHER FOR COMMON ANGLING, OR FLY-FISHING, OR SNAPPING, OR TROLLING . 18

CHAPTER VI.

OF THE BAIT TO BE USED IN SNAPPING OR TROLLING—OF THE MERCILESS METHOD ADOPTED BY SOME FISHERMEN IN USING LIVE BAITS—OF THE SNAP-HOOK, HOW TO BE MADE, AND BAITED, AND USED—FISH TO BE KILLED IMMEDIATELY ON BEING TAKEN, AND WHY—HOW TO TREAT YOUR FISH WHEN YOU HAVE HOOKED HIM AT SNAP . . . . *Page* 22

CHAPTER VII.

UPON TROLLING—THE LINE NOT REQUIRED TO BE SO LARGE AS IN SNAPPING—OF THE HOOK TO BE USED—ALWAYS TO BLUNT THE POINTS—HOW TO TREAT YOUR FISH WHEN YOU HAVE HOOKED HIM AT TROLL—OF THE REEL 30

CHAPTER VIII.

OF TRIMMERS, AND OF THE MOST MERCIFUL WAY OF SETTING THEM, CONTRASTED WITH THE CRUEL METHOD SAID TO HAVE BEEN USED BY SOME FISHERMEN 35

CHAPTER IX.

OF THE COMMON ANGLER—HIS ROD AND LINE—BEST METHOD OF KILLING WORMS BEFORE YOU PUT THEM ON YOUR HOOK . 40

CHAPTER X.

THAT FLY-FISHING STANDS FIRST IN THE ART OF ANGLING—NO *LIVE* FLIES ALLOWED TO BE USED: NOT REQUIRED—OF THE BOOK WHEREIN TO KEEP YOUR FLIES—PROPER FLIES TO BE SELECTED, TAKING YOUR PATTERN FROM THOSE FLIES WHICH FREQUENT THE RIVERS WHERE YOU ARE GOING TO FISH— A GREAT ADVANTAGE TO MAKE YOUR OWN FLIES   45

CHAPTER XI.

HOW TO PREPARE BEFORE YOU COMMENCE MAKING FLIES—FULL DIRECTIONS GIVEN HOW TO MAKE THEM . . . *Page* 49

CHAPTER XII.

THAT IT DOES NOT REQUIRE DELICATE, TAPERING FINGERS TO MAKE FLIES—EXEMPLIFIED IN THE CASE OF A FIRST-RATE FLY-FISHER WHOSE HANDS AND FINGERS WERE REMARKABLY CLUMSY—FISHING WITH *LIVE* MAY-FLIES OR DRAKES CONDEMNED, BEING NOT ONLY CRUEL, BUT QUITE UNNECESSARY—HOW TO THROW YOUR LINES IN WINDY WEATHER AND AT ALL OTHER TIMES—WITH A FEW OBSERVATIONS IN CONCLUSION 58

THE ART OF FISHING.

CHAPTER I.

REMARKS ON NETS AND TACKLE TO BE USED IN FISHING, BUT PRINCIPALLY ON THE CASTING NET—HOW TO TAKE UP AND DELIVER.

HOWEVER FORTUNATE some fishermen may be in catching fish with bad apparatus, yet I lay it down as a general rule, that the best nets, rods, lines, and hooks should be provided, would you enjoy the delightful recreation of fishing.

When I speak of nets, I would not be understood to allow the use of any others, in a general way, than a "casting net" and a "landing net;" the former with which to catch baits, and the latter to lift the fish out of the water when hooked.

I would not, however, be too particular, and

forbid the use of the " bow or hoop net " to catch tench in the months of May and June—the only time of the year, perhaps, when they are on the move; because, in rivers especially, these choice fish are seldom taken without some such process. I say the same, again, of the "flew net," to be set across the stream at the same time of the year, and left to stand a few hours, to catch these fish.

I will now speak of the " casting net."

Its circumference should be from twelve to fourteen yards; not too heavily leaded, that you may cast it the farther, if required; and observe, that the smaller or lighter the net, the longer should be your line—say, twenty yards at least.

In catching baits, it often happens that you must have strength of arm, and length of line, sufficient (unless the river be very broad) to cast your net to the centre of the stream; as the baits or small fry immediately rush towards the current on your approach to the water, and will be soon out of reach unless you be very quick and adroit at this art, more especially if the water be clear. From ten to fifteen yards from the bank of the river you must have the net ready on your arm; and, if possible, the sun in front of you, that your shadow may not frighten the fish when you approach. In throwing, avoid casting your net too high in the air, for this gives the fish more time to escape before it reaches the water: the net ought not to rise higher than midway of your person, nor yet so high if the bank of the stream be elevated.

Let your net fall flat on the water, as this confounds the fish, they not knowing which way to rush first; whereas, if part of your net strikes the water before the other part, they will naturally fly from the splash, and escape before the rest of the net reaches the bottom. All this you must acquire by practice.

I would now lay down a few rules how to take up the casting net, and how to deliver it. And observe by the way that, next to the art of fly-fishing, you must reckon this of *throwing a net*, when properly managed, among the most graceful and elegant of amusements—in fact, I may almost say accomplishments; but it must be properly managed, for you may otherwise reduce it to a vulgar display of clumsy effort, as witnessed in those fishermen who handle the casting net as if it were a shawl to spread over their back and shoulder, where it is laid with the accompaniments of mud and weeds, and the dirty water left to trickle down their sides and legs, to the destruction of coat, waistcoat, and trousers; and in this trim, with their shoes full of dirty water, they swing themselves round like a coal-heaver, and with a *sudden* jerk plunge the net into the water in

A COAL-HEAVER MAKING AN EXPERIMENT IN FISHING.

form more like an oblong, or square, or triangle, or half-moon, than a circle. Now the following method combines ease and elegance with efficiency.

The experienced artist first adjusts his net, and takes especial care that, in drawing it towards him on the ground, the leads are not entangled; that it approaches him perfectly level, the leads being in their proper places like the teeth of the daisy rake. He gathers the line in ringlets, not too large, till he comes to the net, which he gathers in folds (as rings would be liable to entangle and spoil his throw); according to his height he gathers his net long or short, in his left hand (as a general rule, till he comes to about two feet and a half of the bottom), being very careful that his net lies level; he then with his right hand (the line being fastened by a noose on the wrist of his left, with which he grasps the net) takes a very small quantity of the net on the right side, and *gracefully* places it on the tip end of his left elbow, which he elevates to a level nearly with his forehead, to prevent the net slipping off or the water dripping on his shoes; he then begins to gather the net with his right hand (now at liberty), and commences at the lead line on the right close to the other hand (which is grasping the net) placing his little finger on the lead line, and then gathering with the other three fingers and his thumb, till he has rather more than half the remainder of the net in that hand;

he now stands up erect and poises the net; then gently leaning his body to the right, as, pendulum fashion and with as much truth and evenness, he backwards and forwards swings the net, and then

THROWING A CASTING NET.

lets it *flow* off his shoulders with an easy spread, greatly facilitated by a slight obstruction occasioned by the little finger on the lead line, and completes his work by a perfect circle on the water. To effect this with certainty requires great art. I therefore recommend the beginner to practise throwing on a grass plat. As regards the above directions, you must not forget to keep both your elbows elevated, and your hands as near each other as you well can, to avoid everything like a jerk or violence when you cast: in fact, you must study to acquire an easy, graceful, flowing spread in delivering the net, and your object will be gained.

The above plan, if rigidly followed, will not only secure your success in becoming an adept in throwing, but will also save you many a wet skin, spare your clothes, and prevent cold, rheumatism, or ague. Were you attired in your best clothes, you might on the above principle safely catch your baits without wetting any part of them, except at the extreme point of your elbow, and that but slightly if your net be thoroughly wrung. No part of the net should be allowed to touch your clothes, except at the extreme point of your elbow, as I have mentioned. Yet even this can be avoided by the following method:—Place the little finger of your left hand on the lead line, near to that part you generally put on the tip of your elbow, and do not put your net on your elbow at all, and practise throwing in this manner. If the net be a small and light one, you will make nearly as good throws as if you had placed it on your elbow; but the plan is not so certain.

These instructions cannot be considered complete without a caution, not to be in a hurry to draw the net out of the water after you shall have cast it; otherwise the fish, and especially a large fish, may escape underneath the net, for such fish are sure to make a plunge to the bottom. By allowing the net to remain a minute or two before commencing to draw it out of the water, this allows the fish, in their efforts to escape, time to find the tucks, and to retreat into them. In drawing the net to land, let this be performed gradually, and in measured manner, from side to side, which helps to enclose the fish in the tucks. When the net nears the bank or edge of the water, it is a safer process to compress the net in your right hand, beginning from the top till you reach the bottom, holding the bottom as close to the tucks and lead line as may be, lifting the net gently out of the water, and on no account with a swing or jerk, being careful also to withdraw the net some ten or twelve yards from the side of the river. Let the fish be taken out of the net in a quiet, and gentle, and orderly manner, to prevent cruelty. All the sticks, stones, and weeds, if any, should be removed; all mud should be washed clean away, and the net thoroughly wrung, avoiding all extra stamping with the feet on the lower part of it. After each time of using let the net be quite dry, and put away in a dry place: a box is preferable, especially where rats frequent the spot.*

* Would you procure a good casting net, I strongly recommend *Messrs. Mathews and Gent*, Trinity Street, Cambridge. From no part of the kingdom, not even from London itself, could I ever meet with casting nets comparable to theirs for workmanship and management of the widening stitch—the latter so adjusted as to make the throwing of them perfect from the hands of a good artist.

CHAPTER II.

OF THE "LANDING NET"—HOW IT SHOULD BE MADE AND HOW CARRIED.

The "landing net" you must select according to the style of fishing you are going about. If it should be common angling, for trout, perch, roach and dace, it may be made of fine twine, the meshes about three-quarters of an inch diameter, and its depth fifteen inches; the opening, one foot across, and in length fifteen inches, made to screw on a staff three feet long. Some persons, to lengthen the staff, screw one staff into another, which makes it easier to carry when not so attached.

Be sure that the hoop of your landing net be not of iron, as this construction will make your net unnecessarily heavy. I know it is a common practice to make the hoop of this material, but *lance wood* is far better, neater, and lighter.

Should you be going to troll or snap for pike, a landing net of the following description is preferable. Let the hoop, like the former described, be of lance wood. The twine should be very coarse, and very close, that the hooks may not penetrate it when you are landing your fish.

The diameter of the meshes should be an inch and a half, and the depth of the net eighteen inches. If your twine were fine, and the meshes small, your snap hooks would get so entangled by the struggles of your captured fish that you would have great difficulty in undoing them—lose much time, and often to the destruction of your net; for fine twine will not long endure the twisting of a large and powerful pike.

Should you be fishing without a servant or boy to carry your "traps," I recommend the following method to carry your landing net. Have two rings on the staff, one about three inches from the hoop, and the other about two feet below it. Through these rings run a strap, sufficiently long to pass over your shoulder, under your arm, to button slightly in front, that you may in an instant (when you have a bite) loosen the strap with your right hand, which will cause the net to fall on the ground; and the strap, if the rings be not too small, may be instantaneously drawn out, and you will have your net free and ready. Some persons adopt the plan of having a small spear at the bottom of the rod, to enable them to fix it in the ground before they land their fish. I think this a bad plan. I rather advise your holding the rod in your left hand, with the line to bear as tightly on the fish as you dare, till you can tire and land him.

If you once loosen the line (which by using the spear you will be apt to do) before you get your fish into the landing net, you will give him a fair probability of escaping.

The landing net is of a better shape than round at the opening, if the lance wood be formed into the shape of a pear.

CHAPTER III.

OF THE "HOOP OR BOW NET"—ITS SIZE—HOW TO SET AND HOW TO BAIT IT.

We come now to speak of the hoop or bow net, useful to catch tench in the months of May and June. These nets should be about four feet from hoop to hoop, and their opening about two feet diameter; the meshes about an inch and a half diameter, for general use. But should you wish to catch eels with them (and they generally frequent the same rivers as tench), the meshes of your net must be much smaller. Bow nets should be decorated inside with flowers, or a bunch of them suspended in the middle—honeysuckles I should prefer. To suspend the bunch, tie a small stone in it, which if you properly adjust, the string will hang down in the middle of the net. Without this precaution, the flowers will float, and stick against the top and sides of the net, instead of hanging opposite the centre of the hoops, which they ought to do, to invite the company into Flora's Hall along the netted channel, instead of the party remaining outside to enjoy the bouquet at the sides of the net, without going in; a liberty you must not allow. Be very careful that your net be equally leaded, not heavier at one end than at the other; for if it is, when placed in the river, the heavier side will raise the opposite hoop from the bottom, and mar your success.

As a general rule do not set your net in deep water, but rather by the side of the river; and be careful to set it along the stream, not across it; and set it between the weeds, in those channels you often see at the bottom of rivers. I give this caution, because the fish have regular paths, like the sheep on an open plain. So if you place your nets on the weeds, instead of at the sides of them, the finny travellers may never discover the accommodation provided for them. The sides of bulrushes, and often under projecting banks, are favourite haunts for tench. As a last direction I should recommend that the bow net has never more than two feet of water above it when set; one foot would be better. No water above it, but level with the top, would be most preferable of all. In some rivers you cannot accomplish this with hoop nets of the size I have given; so if the sides of the stream be too deep for the plan I am recommending, you must have your nets of a larger size. Have the splints of your bow net painted green, like the general colour of the weeds:

SETTING THE BOW NET.

strangers will then be more likely to pass by without observing them. And should there be loose weeds near, cover your nets with them; but do not break the weeds up too near your net, for you may destroy the paths I have alluded to, and the fish will not find their way to the net.

CHAPTER IV.

CONTAINS SEVERAL PARTICULARS RELATING TO THE FLEW NET—ITS SIZE—DESCRIBING THE LINT AND WALL—HOW TO SET.

Your "flew net" to catch tench should be in size and length according to the breadth of the river; rather longer than across the stream, that you may set it *loose*. The depth of the net from four to seven feet, as best suits the depth of the river; I limit it to seven feet, because, however deep may be the water you set it across, the lint of your flew will sink down from its weight and magnitude, if the net exceeds seven feet in depth. The corks may support the flew, but the lint will get so straightened that the fish will not entangle themselves in it: the leads should be of sufficient weight to sink the net to the bottom; so, if the river be very deep, you must run the hazard of some of the fish swimming over the corks, which will of course be the case with those fish that swim higher than seven feet from the bottom. The *lint* is the small network of the flew, which should be made of very fine twine, or the fish will not entangle themselves so well; silk is better than twine: in fact, the lint cannot well be too flimsy and fine, if it be strong; it should contain twice the number of square feet as the frame of the flew, in order that the fish may bag themselves when they force it through the wall (as it is called) of the flew. The wall is that part of the net which faces the "*lint*" on both sides, and should be made of coarse twine in squares or large meshes of about five or six inches; the wall to be of the same size as the frame of the flew, in quantity half as much as the lint. The meshes of the lint should be two inches in diameter. Set the net as loose as you well can.

CHAPTER V.

UPON THE CHOICE OF YOUR ANGLE ROD, WHETHER FOR COMMON ANGLING, OR FLY-FISHING, OR SNAPPING, OR TROLLING.

THE fishing-rod, of course, must be adapted to the style of fishing you are going to follow, as to whether it be what is called common angling, or fly-fishing, or trolling, or snapping. These rods should all vary, with this exception—that you might troll with a snapping rod, but not snap with a trolling rod; and for this obvious reason, the latter would be too stiff and clumsy, and your fish would escape from want of that spring and elasticity required in the rod to make the hook penetrate the jaw of the fish when you strike him, a circumstance which has often occurred to me, and which has been followed by the loss of many a good fish; and, besides, the strike should be instantaneous with the biting, which, with a stiff rod (as trolling rods generally are), would not be the case; in consequence the fish escapes. Your common angle rod is the least difficult to select, so long as it is tolerably pliable, and not less than four yards and a half long, which will answer every purpose.

But your fly rod in pliability and shape should be unexceptionable; it should taper from the butt to the top with the greatest truth and nicety, and so should the line taper till you arrive at the fly. Your choice of this rod should be according to your strength; a double-handed rod (which for trout and grayling I should never recommend) is all very well for salmon fishing, or for very broad rivers, but would you study "otium cum dignitate," a figure elegant with dignity and ease, to be reflected in the stream, you must abandon the double-handed rod, and leave it for the use of those whose clumsy gait so ill becomes an art acknowledged to be most graceful.

Your trolling or snapping rod should be four yards and a half long; the latter lighter and more pliable than the former; furnished with stiff rings, in order that the line may run through them more freely, and that you may be enabled to throw your bait at a further distance, thirty yards out, if required. In trolling or snapping from a boat on large meres, or from the sides of broad rivers, you will find it a great advantage to be able to cast your line long distances, especially in the former plan, as the boat will frighten the fish near it.

Endeavour to let the bait fall on the water as lightly as possible; this may be accomplished by checking the line with your right hand just before the bait touches the surface, a dodge acquired by practice, but soon learnt. You should often examine your stiff rings, as they are apt to get jagged from friction, especially from long throws. In this case they will tear or chafe the line, the varnish or composition will wear off, and your line will be weakened, and soon give way. Many persons gather the line in rings before they throw it out; this may answer very well in short casts, but not when you are fishing from a boat, or on the bank, and have to throw twenty or thirty yards; for then the line will not pass freely, but will catch at the rings nine times out of ten. So let the line lie at the bottom of the boat, or on the ground if you are on shore, as you gather it, and be careful that you do not set your foot upon it, as you will be very apt to do in stepping forward to cast; this will spoil your throw, and hamper you exceedingly, especially if you are fishing from a boat. I mention this because I know from experience that unless you are on your guard, you will every now and then be stamping on your line. In snapping, to catch your fish at a great distance from you adds much to the amusement, as then great dexterity is required to strike with precision, and so you *must* strike to secure your prize, for the further the fish is from you, the more difficult it is to hook him, for distance gives time between the biting and the striking.

CHAPTER VI.

OF THE BAIT TO BE USED IN SNAPPING OR TROLLING—OF THE MERCILESS METHOD ADOPTED BY SOME FISHERMEN IN USING LIVE BAITS—OF THE SNAP-HOOK, HOW TO BE MADE, AND BAITED, AND USED—FISH TO BE KILLED IMMEDIATELY ON BEING TAKEN, AND WHY—HOW TO TREAT YOUR FISH WHEN YOU HAVE HOOKED HIM AT SNAP.

YOUR bait, either to troll or snap with, should be a small one; I should say, never larger than a good-sized gudgeon. KILL THE BAIT BEFORE YOU USE IT.*

I am now entering on the merciful mode of angling; and to draw particular attention to this part of the work, I give the first merciful direction in capital letters. "Yes—but, ah!" says one, "there is nothing like a *live bait*." This I deny, and would not fear, were I in the habit of betting, to risk a considerable sum of money that I would with a snap hook, properly baited

---

* Although small baits are recommended as the most killing, yet it does not follow that large ones never answer. I have known an instance of one pike seizing another, somewhat of its own size, and both of them having been found dead in the river—one choked for his greediness, and the other suffocated in the throat of his enemy.

with a *dead* gudgeon, we will say, or any other small fish, equal, if not surpass the success of the merciless angler who impales when alive the poor defenceless little bait, and keeps him writhing on the hook, to entice the ravenous pike, or passes a wire down his back, and thus spits him alive, that he may live the longer on his hook. To avoid this cruelty, for I can call it by no milder name, let your snap-hook be properly baited with a dead gudgeon, or dace, or roach, or with a little trout, this last being the best of all baits. I have said *properly* baited, for there are two ways of putting on your bait, as there are two ways of doing most things, viz. a good and a bad way. Provide yourself with a set of hooks,* size No. 2 or 3, whipped on the gimp (minnow-tackle fashion), three placed back to back, at the extremity of the gimp, three more about an inch or so higher up the gimp, three more about the same distance from the last (all placed back to back); and above all these, a small sliding hook, about No. 6, which you are to put through the lips of the bait; then, with one of the three

* I recommend different sized hooks should your baits be smaller than a gudgeon—say, No. 4 or 5. So you should be provided with different sized snap-hooks, some nearly as small as minnow-tackle, or quite so; for many a good pike has been caught with small hooks.

hooks of the middle set, pierce the bait near the tail, turning the barb upwards, i.e. towards the head of the bait: this will bend the fish's tail, and cause it to resist the water as you draw it up and down, or across the stream. This process gives it a spinning motion, and the appearance of a *live* bait; and so rapid will be this movement if you have two swivels on your line, that it will *sparkle* in the water, and probably attract the pike from a far greater distance than a live bait would.

Unless the water should be very deep, let your bait, when spinning, be about five or six inches from the surface; you will then see it, if the water be tolerably clear, and it should be so if you expect to catch fish in this way. Seeing the bait is certainly an advantage, as you can then at once distinguish between the obstruction of a weed and a bite; for the pike will be sure to show himself, turning his white body upwards, which he must do in order to seize the bait, from the shortness of his under jaw. When you shall have hooked him, should he be a small fish, say under two pounds weight, do not unbuckle your landing net, but drag him out at once, as it were by the hair of his head (if he had any); for your snapping tackle ought to be sufficiently strong to land a fish of that weight without a landing net. KILL THE FISH DIRECTLY YOU SHALL HAVE CAUGHT HIM.

Be provided with a staff, about a foot long, which you can carry in your side pocket; with this smite the fish with a smart blow on the back of his head, close to the neck, and he will be dead in an instant. You may then take the hooks out of his mouth, but not before—would you follow the merciful directions given in the present work. Besides, he might bite your fingers if not dead, from the pain you would give him in extracting the hooks; and it is the hearty wish of the author that he may, if you are so cruel as to torture him unnecessarily. By killing your fish at once, you not only curtail his suffering, but you secure to yourself a better fish. For fish killed on the instant they are caught eat firmer than when left to die a lingering death. Should you wish to know why, I will tell you. And may the information work on the feelings of those merciless fishermen who leave their fish, when caught, to die by slow degrees, either half smothered in their panniers, or strung on a stick, with their torn and bleeding gills hanging down their tormentors' sides. A fish which dies by degrees, wastes itself; and why? FROM PAIN AND SUFFERING!

If you observe them, they seem to sigh, their

flesh becomes flabby—so much so, that when they are dressed, they have in a measure lost that firmness which a sudden death, like that I have mentioned, would have spread over the whole fish. The blow has somewhat the same effect as in the cod-fish when crimped, and without the torture which this choice fish must suffer in having his back and sides lacerated when alive, and left to die in agony; a cruelty uncalled for, as the same effect might be produced would the operator strike the cod on the nose before crimping him, and thus kill him, for instant death is the consequence of a blow on that part of the fish. Thus there are two reasons why the fish, captured whether by net or hook, should be killed immediately—the more important of the two, that he suffers no unnecessary pain; the other, less important, that he will eat the better.

In catching pike with rod and line, I have treated specially on snapping, because it is the plan I generally adopt in preference to trolling, and from its being the more merciful plan of the two. Both methods, however, may come under the denomination of "trolling," the word troll signifying "to walk," as you may walk, and even run, in the exercise of this art. However, for distinction sake, we will consider it trolling when we fish with a gorge hook, and snapping when the bait is not swallowed, but the fish struck immediately on its biting. On this latter plan I would make a few more observations before I enter on the subject of trolling. Should you see your fish seize the bait (which in all probability you will by adopting the plan I have been recommending, that is, by keeping the bait within six inches from the surface of the water), strike him the contrary way to his head, that you may not pull the hooks and bait out of his mouth: should you, however, not see him bite, strike upwards. I have already given directions how to treat him then, if hooked, should he be a small fish; but if, on the contrary, he should prove to be a large one, which you will at once find him to be (even if you do not see him) should he bear heavy on your rod, let him run a few yards, keeping your rod tolerably tight, so as to feel him tug, raising him at the same time gradually towards the surface, strictly on your guard lest the line should be too tight while this process is going on, as a sudden dash of the fish might in that case break it. In fact, in snapping you must never let the fish carry your line from you without difficulty on his part, letting him know that you have him *in tow*, yet careful not to hold him too tightly, to the breaking either of rod or line, or both; which a powerful fish might do if not *judiciously* managed. When you get him to the surface, there let him play and roll over, again and again, which in all probability he will do; for the higher you raise him in the water the more he will tire himself, till at the last you can drag him to the side, and take him out with the landing net. When you have him safe on shore, place him *immediately* (for he will then be tired, and will lie *still* for a few seconds) on the ground, with his back upwards. Out with your staff, and strike him with a sharp blow on the nape of his neck, close to his head, after the manner already given; as to a smaller fish, he will not require a second blow if he opens his mouth and leaves it in a *contracted* state, which is a sure sign of sudden death. Put him in your pannier with some fresh grass, not with hay, as with that he would dry too fast, and lose his beauty before you got him home to show him to your friends. Both in snapping and trolling, look well to your lines that they be strong. You cannot well adopt a more merciless mode of angling than to fish with *weak or rotten lines*. The very thought of a fish breaking away from you, either with a gorged bait or his jaws centracted with a double hook, should make you most careful in the examination of your lines, as in the former instance the fish must in all probability pine away with internal pain and suffering, and in the latter by starvation.

CHAPTER VII.

UPON TROLLING—THE LINE NOT REQUIRED TO BE SO LARGE AS IN SNAPPING—OF THE HOOK TO BE USED—ALWAYS TO BLUNT THE POINTS—HOW TO TREAT YOUR FISH WHEN YOU HAVE HOOKED HIM AT TROLL—OF THE REEL.

THE art of trolling comes now under our consideration, a much easier art than that of snapping, although it requires great nicety and careful fishing to secure success; such as casting the bait, sometimes at a great distance from you, and in that case to let the bait fall lightly on the water, as the greater the distance you cast, the more you add to that difficulty. For directions in casting your line, see the article on Snapping, page 24. Your line should be much smaller, say by half, than your snapping line; for no great strength is required to hold your fish when he shall have gorged the bait, you giving him sufficient time to run at his pleasure. Your hook should be a double one, though perhaps a single one might answer the purpose, and possibly less likely to prevent the pike from swallowing the bait. The hook, whether double or single, should have a piece of lead along the shank, not too heavy, and for these reasons: that it will fall with less noise on the water, and that the pike will be more likely to gorge the bait when he has taken it. Indeed, very killing fishermen often troll without any lead whatever on their hook. I, however, prefer a small quantity of lead, were it only to enable me to cast the line further, and to make the bait sink faster.

"But what becomes of the mercy you speak of, "if you use a gorge bait or hook?" I hear the cavilling fisherman exclaim. To which I reply— *comparative mercy* is what I undertake to prove may be shown in every branch of fishing; so much so, as to make this fascinating sport, comparatively, a merciful amusement as placed beside the other sports of the day. Be careful to blunt the hooks before you use them, in order to lessen the pain of your captured (or to be captured) fish after he has swallowed the bait, which is best done with a file; blunt them effectually, sufficiently so to admit of their being pressed on your hands without piercing them. You may be just as likely, yea, more so, to catch a pike than if the points of the hook were sharp, as in the latter instance the fish will often, and very often, prick himself when he bites, and leave the bait, to be trusted no more. Avoid the unmerciful plan of *striking* the fish when you think he has swallowed the bait; for if your hooks are well formed, a little projecting from the mouth of the bait, the hook when gorged will hold your fish, and probably without any jerk whatever. Be *tender* throughout the whole process of securing him, and let him tire himself without your pulling and lugging him about; and, in trolling, never land him, whether he be small or great, without a landing net, or taking him carefully out of the water with your hands—but not by putting your fingers in his eyes, a method recommended by some barbarous anglers.

Instantly kill him when taken, as recommended for all captured fish.

When you have a bite, slacken your line as much as possible, and be careful that nothing obstructs its running freely. When the line stops, wait at least five minutes before you disturb your fish: in all probability, if he shall have swallowed the bait, he will move off again before that time shall have expired, and perhaps he will rise to the surface, spring out of the water, and shake himself, endeavouring to disgorge the bait, which he will do nine times out of ten; but not the hook or hooks. Some pike, according to their size, will run out from ten to thirty or forty yards. When the five minutes shall have expired, and no movement, very gently pull your line, and feel, by that means, whether the fish has left your bait or not: should he still retain it, he will run off again; and if he has not already gorged it, will probably do so in five minutes more, if he intends to do it at all. I should therefore say that the time altogether, allowing for circumstances, would not exceed a quarter of an hour between his biting and your landing him, or his biting and perhaps spoiling your bait, and wishing you good-day, not accepting your *polite* invitation to dinner, or to appear at your board. I have said nothing as to the method of baiting your gorge-hook: it is so simple, that I need perhaps hardly observe that the gimp or arming wire should be drawn through the bait from the mouth to the tail, till the double or single hook fits in between the lips of the bait. Some persons tie the tail of the bait fish to the arming wire or gimp, to prevent its slipping up the line.

Try short throws first; and let out more line by degrees, till you can throw your utmost limit without leaving the place where you stand. Cast up and down, and across the river, without moving from the spot till you shall have fished as far as you can reach.

Upon the subject of trolling and snapping, little more need be said than has been already laid down in this and the foregoing chapter, save only perhaps as regards the reel, which, to prevent the line from ever entangling, should be a very simple one; certainly not brass, with the wheel enclosed (the old-fashioned pattern): it should be, on the contrary, a naked wheel, with a broad circumference, wherein should be cut a groove sufficiently wide to hold a line of about thirty-five or forty yards or more long. Box-wood perhaps would be the best to make it of. Your line should have a portion of hair in it, whether it be silk or twine, that it may not stick to your rod in wet weather, and it should be prepared with a sort of copal varnish.

CHAPTER VIII.

OF TRIMMERS, AND OF THE MOST MERCIFUL WAY OF SETTING THEM, CONTRASTED WITH THE CRUEL METHOD SAID TO HAVE BEEN USED BY SOME FISHERMEN.

MANY trollers and snappers are fond now and then of setting trimmers, a name they may well be called by; for they are often *trimmers* indeed, not only to the poor unfortunate *live* baits with which they are often set, but to the equally unfortunate hooked pike, which, for many hours, even days and nights, are customarily left to swim about with the hooks in their entrails. Of course this cruel method of catching fish would not be countenanced in a work like the present. If a trimmer must be set, let it be *watched*, at least, not left, but for a short time; not baited with a *live* bait, for that is unnecessary.

If it is at all a *biting* day (and why fish if it should not be so?), a fresh killed bait, and immediately put on the hook, will be sufficiently inviting to the prowling fresh-water *wolf* (as the pike is aptly called) to prevail upon him to seize his prey. This I know from experience. A pike may be as much directed or drawn towards the bait by the sense of *smelling* as by that of *seeing*. This seems to account for your not often having sport with an artificial bait, made, as we see them at the present day, to perfection; and this reminds me, by the way, that should you ever be fishing with an artificial bait, rub it every now and then with a fresh killed dead fish: the deception probably becomes heightened, as you may thus deceive your prey in two of his senses instead of in one.

I have said, as regards the trimmer, let it be watched, or not left, but for a short time, that if it be sprung, you may at once or very soon release by death any suffering the captured fish may be exposed to. Following this plan, and if the hooks be blunted as recommended in trolling, and the fish lifted out of the water with a landing net or by your hands, there will be no more suffering than in the way described above. However, I am no friend to trimmers, nor would allow more than one, or two, or three, to be used at a time: you could watch one, or go back to it now and then when trolling; whereas, if several be set, your looking after them would too much interfere with your other sport.

As a contrast to the comparative mercy of setting a trimmer in the way I have been showing, is the following method; practised, as I have been credibly informed, by whom I know not, nor do I wish to know—a brute, and worse, with two legs, which is a far milder name than such an operator deserves, who catches a frog, scrapes his back with a knife, and sprinkles him with *aqua fortis,* to make him shriek and cry out, when thus put upon the hook, and thrown on the water, to entice his enemy the pike to come and devour him!

"*Contemplation and action,*" says Isaac Walton, "*are combined in the art of angling.*" If the above cruel process be the action, what must the contemplation be? Let us hope that no one, save a thoughtless, uncontemplative person, could resort to such a cruel, merciless, and surely we may add *fiendish* method of pastime.

Although we may have drawn a highly coloured picture in the manner of setting a trimmer, yet it serves to show what a difference exists in the way you may set about it compared with the merciful way I have been recommending.

Careful management and a little extra trouble

might not only reduce the amusement of fishing to *comparative mercy*, but greatly add to the enjoyment of the sport, to find that your varied endeavours to free your victims from all unnecessary pain and suffering had been successful. Indeed, from want of this careful management, fishing has acquired a bad name, and has been branded as the most cruel of all diversions. Divest it of all *unnecessary* suffering, it stands forth, as we have said, by far the least cruel of all sports.

We have confined ourselves, thus far, to those departments of the art which relate to the casting net; the hoop, landing, and flew nets; to snapping and trolling with rod and line; and to the setting of the trimmer. We fear not to pursue this recreation through more of its branches, and to show how simply we may avoid giving pain and suffering, *comparatively* considered, to the fish we endeavour to capture, or to those baits we use for that purpose.

In common angling, with worms, I conceive it to be most difficult, with all our care, to avoid giving pain both to the bait and the fish. Alleviation may be carried out to a very great extent, sufficiently to make the pain short as regards the worm as well as the hooked fish;

being only for a few seconds. This shall be shown after giving directions to the common angler, whom I describe by this appellation to distinguish " him " from the troller, the snapper, and the fly-fisher.

CHAPTER IX.

OF THE COMMON ANGLER—HIS ROD AND LINE—BEST METHOD OF KILLING WORMS BEFORE YOU PUT THEM ON YOUR HOOK.

THE common angler should provide himself with a rod of the description given, page 18. The line should be longer than the rod—not quite half so long again, as a general rule;* for if it be longer it will be difficult to cast, and the hook will be every now and then catching the ground or rushes on the bank, while you are endeavouring to throw it out. The line, as in snapping or trolling, should not be all of silk, but some hair should be mixed with it, or else, as in the above style of fishing, it will be apt to stick to the rod in rainy weather. Have about a yard or so of gut attached to your hook, with about three or four, or more, split shot on it, according to the size of your

* It is a very good plan to angle with your trolling line, as you can then let out, and draw in, as much of your line as you please. Besides, with the help of the reel, if you carry a float in your pocket, you can at any time change your style of fishing from pike to perch.

float. Plumb the depth of water before you begin to fish. If angling for perch, have your hook six inches from the bottom; if for float fish, roach, dace, or bleak, about the same distance from the top. For the former, bait with a worm; but for the latter, with dough and bread crumbs, mixed with a little honey or sugar, and kneaded with a small quantity of cotton wool, as the wool will make the composition stick longer on your hook, and not waste by absorption in the water. Your hook for perch should be No. 3 or 4; for float fishing, about No. 9, and even as small as No. 11 or 12, especially if there be bleak in the stream.* I pass over any further directions as to this method of angling; it is so common, and so much has been written on the subject, that

* It might be objected to this work, that nothing is said in it about the celebrated art of fly-fishing for salmon, considered, as I know it is, by many anglers, to stand first in the list for fly-fishing, which I believe to be a great mistake. The salmon is often a stubborn and obstinate fish to deal with when hooked. After his first run out, notwithstanding all your care, he will often locate himself by the side of a rock or large stone at the bottom, and, in defiance of all your art to remove him, will remain there for hours. Not so the trout, who will play from first to last, with a small degree of care on your part to keep him near the surface (p. 67). Besides, the art of angling for salmon is omitted on the same principle as the art of angling for several other fish—the carp, the grayling, and the barbel, for instance—the purport of this work being to show the most merciful mode of catching fish *in general.*

it would be superfluous to say anything more; and the same observation must apply to angling (common angling, I mean) for any other fish than those I have mentioned.

My province lies principally concerning the *most merciful way* of proceeding, and of this I shall now treat.

Before you place the worm * on your hook, place it on the palm of your right hand; throw it then on the ground, as hard as you well can. Were you to take it in your fingers, and in this way cast the worm on the ground, it would not fall so evenly nor so hardly. The worm, by the method I recommend, will become at once *paralysed* and constricted. Instantly nip off his head, and run your hook down his full length till the barb reaches his tail. "Yes, this may be all very

---

* The worm should be tolerably transparent, free from anything like dirt, either outside or inside; it should also be very tough and elastic. You must not expect to get such worms as these from your garden ground or from dung-heaps the day you go fishing: they must be collected at least a fortnight or ten days previously, and put into a common large brown milkpan with plenty of clean damp moss, and fed with a little cream sprinkled on it every day or two; and the moss should be washed before you repeat the sprinkling of the cream. Without this preparation your worms will break, and the dirt ooze out of them. When thrown hard on the ground, as instructed, they should be killed.

The benefit of washing the moss every now and then is to take away the sourness of the cream before you add fresh cream.

"well," says the heartless angler, "but give me "a live worm, that wriggles about the hook when "pierced, and thus tempts the finny tribe." Hear me in reply:—Provide yourself with a little bottle of anise-seed oil. Dip your hook, when baited after my plan, in the oil, and commence fishing. Should it happen to be a biting day, and should there be a good store of perch, the probabilities will be, you will certainly surpass, or at least equal, the merciless angler. The odds would be as six to four in favour of the angler who uses anise-seed oil, in a party of anglers. "But as to "the fish you may have hooked, and have swallowed "your bait, what becomes of your mercy to "your greedy customers?" I hear the caviller rejoin. I reply, it is true they must suffer, but there is no need that their sufferings should be beyond momentary. Immediately on your float sinking from a bite, you pull out your victim. Should he be a perch under half a pound weight, you ought not to lose a moment in thrusting your thumb down his throat, and bending his head backwards, and thus break his neck. Should he be a larger fish, have your staff ready, and, according to former directions, give him a smart blow on the back of his neck; *then* take out the hook, but not before. Should the fish you may have hooked be too large to pull out on a sudden, use your landing net, as previously directed, and do not gradually draw him up the bank, with his weight telling on the hook in his entrails. In every instance kill your fish when taken.*

The above directions may apply to all fish taken with the angle, in the common way of angling. They are merciful directions, and, if strictly followed, would save from pain and suffering the poor writhing worm, "humble, silent, "innocent, overlooked, oppressed, and trodden "under foot," and likewise many a struggle of the captured fish. Far from blunting our feelings when we commence a day's angling, we should call them up in full force, and study through the whole of our pastime to exercise the tenderest mercy that circumstances will permit; and this, as we have hinted, is the true way to enjoy our sport.

As to night-lines, ledger baits, left for several hours in succession, and eel gores jagged to hold the struggling prey, we discard all these methods of catching fish, as not only heartless and cruel, but partaking very largely of the nature of poaching. They hold no place in this work, or countenance.

---

* The repetition " to kill your fish immediately on being "taken" must not offend the critical observer, for in fact it is the *chorus* of this little work.

CHAPTER X.

THAT FLY-FISHING STANDS FIRST IN THE ART OF ANGLING—NO LIVE FLIES ALLOWED TO BE USED: NOT REQUIRED—OF THE BOOK WHEREIN TO KEEP YOUR FLIES—PROPER FLIES TO BE SELECTED, TAKING YOUR PATTERN FROM THOSE FLIES WHICH FREQUENT THE RIVERS WHERE YOU ARE GOING TO FISH—A GREAT ADVANTAGE TO MAKE YOUR OWN FLIES.

WE pass on now to give a few directions in the charming, fascinating, and delightful art of fly-fishing. Connected with angling this stands foremost. In pursuing the object of a work like this, the motto of which is "Mercy blended with "pity," it is hailed with no small satisfaction. For be it understood that we allow no *live* flies to be used, but simply artificial flies, for they are not required, which shall be proved as we proceed in our enquiry.

The rod and line to be used are described at page 19. You should provide yourself with a book, the leaves of which should be faced with a slight surface of cotton wool, or wadding, that you may so hang your flies on it as to admit of their being taken off conveniently, without every now and then undoing the coils, in which they are generally put up in dozens and half-dozens.

Be very careful to select your flies, the hooks of which have small gut attached to them (unless you intend them for bob or side-flies), smaller than the end of that part of the gut on which you attach your fly gut, and the smaller the fly the smaller should be your gut. If the master of the fishing-tackle shop where you purchase your tackle should happen to be a fly-fisherman himself (which is often the case), you may expect to get your necessary apparatus in proper order and trim. Some fly-fishermen have the corners of the leaves of their books for flies headed with a small piece of flat cork; this, generally speaking, I think perfectly unnecessary if the leaves have a shallow woollen surface as I have described. The flat cork method is intended to prevent the flies from being pressed, but my plan is much better, being neater and taking up less room, as the flies when the book is closed will sink into the wool, and avoid pressure. The cork plan may answer very well for stout flies, such as the May or Drake fly, so you may have one or two of the leaves of your book furnished with cork fittings. The variety in flies is so various, as also are the tastes of the fish you endeavour to catch, that it is absolutely necessary (unless you would throw away your money and time) to find out what sort of flies frequent the rivers you are going to fish.

"But how am I to know this?" says the inexperienced artist. One way, and a wise way, is to buy your flies in the neighbourhood of the river you are going to fish, at the nearest town. This, however, I know, is not always to be done; yet on most streams you meet with knowing hands, who would supply you with a few patterns, some of which you might forward to London by the post, have them made to perfection, and sent before those given to you were worn out. Should your stay be short on any particular stream, write beforehand and get the proper flies from the neighbourhood of the river, at least a pattern or two, that you may have them made up before you leave your home. Would you wish to have them made to perfection, I strongly recommend FARLEY, in the Strand, whose shop is furnished with fishing tackle of exquisite workmanship, and who is a noted fisherman.

I have been rather particular in the above directions, knowing from experience that unless your flies be of the sort that frequent the river you fish in, your labour, if not in vain, will be very little rewarded; ten to one against you at least. I shall now in the ensuing chapter recommend a plan which will entirely do away with the trouble above stated, add considerably to the sport—in truth double the pleasure. The plan is: MAKE YOUR OWN FLIES.

CHAPTER XI.

HOW TO PREPARE BEFORE YOU COMMENCE MAKING FLIES—FULL DIRECTIONS GIVEN HOW TO MAKE THEM.

How to make flies is an art of itself, and practised by many who are not fishermen; which brings me to the following conclusion, that you may be a good fly-maker and yet a bad fisherman, but certainly not a good and an accomplished fisherman and a bad fly-maker. You must overcome the difficulty of making flies, or you will never know the real pleasure a good fly-fisherman experiences in the exercise of his art.

To catch a fish with a fly of your own manufacture, or with a fly made by another person, produces two opposite feelings; somewhat like the pleasure or indifference which an admirer of the fine arts experiences in beholding a picture as an original or a copy, or the satisfaction or dissatisfaction which the Divine experiences in preaching another man's sermon or his own. It is true, the two latter may both catch men, but the capture will be more satisfactory if effected by one's own tackle.

To make your own flies, you must be provided with a set of hooks of different sizes, varying from No. 3 to 12, and smaller still if you can procure them. Your gut should be very small—small, I say —in all patterns, to suit the fly to which it is attached (except in the case of bob or side-flies), at the extremity of the tapering from the very butt end of your rod; the gut for your end-fly (I call it so to distinguish from the bob or side-fly) should be from eight to ten inches long, not shorter, that the joining on may not be too near your fly. You must procure dubbing of different colours. Some persons recommend wools dyed for that purpose. I see, however, no general necessity for this; Nature being the best dyer. Get together the following wools, and soft hair, so fine as to resemble the down on feathers, the former from the neck and under part of the sheep, that it may be the softer and finer, the latter from the inside of the ears of horses of different colours; from donkeys' ears also. In fact dubbing may be procured from various animals; from the red and white spaniel for instance, from the fox or polecat, also from stoats, weasels, and ferrets. By a careful selection you may obtain dubbing of various colours, sufficient for your purpose, according to the variety of animals you take it from. Such dubbing will not change colour from the influence of water, as the dyed wool may be liable to do; also it may be more deceptive. If you cannot arrive quite so near to the colour of the pattern before you from the use only of the natural wool, the probabilities are that the difficulty will be supplied, getting as near as may be; and that your fly, when made, will be quite as killing. Many persons are very particular in the colour of the silk they use in whipping on the hook, that it may resemble the natural fly in colour. This I think needless, because the dubbing placed on the silk will conceal its colour. You should have a proper dubbing book, arranged in little slides to slip into the leaves, both slides to be made of parchment. Number the slides according to the colour of your dubbing. With this book before you on a table, with a proper supply of hooks and gut, with feathers also taken from the neck of the game cock to make your hackles, and other feathers from various birds, as from the wings of a landrail, or in default of them from the partridge's tail—these you will find very useful to make the wings of a fly. Besides these, pigeons' feathers, as well as those from the woodcock or dotterel, will be found useful. Other sorts might be mentioned, but the fewer the better in order to simplify the process of fly-making. Be sure to select your feathers from the wild bird whenever you can, which are brighter and certainly stiffer, and therefore not so likely to become flabby in the water. So do not use the feathers from the common barn-door cock, or the bantam, nor yet those of the tame pigeon or drake. The wings of the May fly made with the feathers from the breast of the tame drake will not resist the water, but collapse and stick to the sides of the fly; whereas those from the mallard or wild drake, having more stiffness in them, will recover their position after having been drawn across the stream. The same observation will apply as regards the hackle which you bind round the body of your fly. The hackle of the game cock will remain stiff, and retain its natural appearance, and show itself till your fly is worn out, like the body of the caterpillar in the broad sun, whereas other hackle from the tamer brood will be liable to stick to the body of your fly and impair its deceptive qualities. You should also avoid using the feathers from young birds, for the same reason, as they will not be sufficiently stiff. Before you make the wings of the drake or May fly, boil the feathers in turmeric, which will turn them yellow, for that is the natural colour of that fly. You should also have ready before you, on a table placed as near the window as possible, and yourself seated with the light full in your face, a small pair of sharp scissors, pointed; some wax on a small piece of parchment (that you may hold it between your finger and thumb when waxing, without getting any on your fingers); some fine silk, with your hackle ready prepared, and that after the following method :—Split your silk, that it may be as fine as possible; taking one of the strands, which should be five or six inches long, and wax it carefully—I say carefully, because in consequence of your having removed it from the other strands it will be very weak, and liable to break; and when you have waxed it, double a small portion of the end of it, as if you were going to tie a knot in it, leaving it not drawn close, but sufficient room left to insert the tip end of your hackle, clipping a little of the feather off at the root first; this done, tie the knot tightly after you shall have inserted the tip end of the feather into it. In order to effect this, you must first of all hold the tip end of the hackle or feather between the thumb and finger of your *left* hand, and with the thumb and finger of your *right* hand turn the feathers back till you make them stick out like porcupine's quills, or a chimney-sweeper's brush.

We will now suppose the above articles on the table before you (together with a needleful of silk, ready waxed), that is to say, the hook, the gut, the feathers for the fly's wings, the hackle with the fine strand of silk attached to it as just directed, the scissors, the dubbing (the latter selected from your book, to match the colour of the fly you wish to make). Everything necessary to your purpose being ready, take the hook between the finger and thumb of your *left* hand, having the barb turned downwards; now, with your *right* hand, take up the needleful of waxed silk, and whip it round the shank of the hook, about four or five coils only, leaving about the sixteenth of an inch between each coil; then upon the shank of your hook and on the coils lay the gut; commence whipping again, very close and fine, till you shall have fastened on the hook. You will, of course, have plenty of the above needleful of silk left, and ready waxed. Now then, holding your hook as before in your left hand, take up some dubbing with your right hand in small quantity, and with the finger and thumb of the same hand rub it on three or four inches of the waxed silk which is to spare, and with which you are making the fly; and when you shall have put as much dubbing on the silk as you may judge sufficient to complete the body of your fly, commence whipping again with the silk, and its dubbing on it, and thus form the body. Tie it closely. Then place the root end of the hackle on the end of the shank of the hook, and tie it down closely with the silk you shall have been whipping with; then take hold of the strand of the fine silk at the tip end of your hackle, and wind the feather carefully round the body of the fly till you arrive nearly to the bend of the hook, tying it down closely with the strand of the fine silk fastened on it, and cut away the remainder of that fine silk, and your fly is so far completed without its wings, and becomes what is called a palmer fly. Now, according to the size of the pattern fly before you, or of the fly you wish to make, take a small quantity of the feathers for the fly's wings as already directed, and lying before you: divide the portion you take up into two equal parts, placing one part on the right, and the other on the left of the body of your fly, near to its head, making them stick up; then fasten them down with the remainder of your silk, and cut away the rest of your silk which may have remained, and your fly is completed.

It is extremely difficult to give directions for fly-making in *writing*—I mean sufficiently so to make an accomplished artist. Directions in writing, after having seen a fly made, will wonderfully forward you in the art. I therefore strongly recommend your seeing the process, and watching narrowly the method resorted to by a good fly-maker, before you study my directions.

It is for the making a very simple fly that I have laid down the above rules. To avoid making those rules too complicated, I have left out accompaniments in fly-making, of making horns, tails, gold and silver twist for the bodies of flies, which you must use, when required, in tying down your dubbing, before you wind round your hackle. As an instance, before you tie down at the bend of your hook, place the tail on it, which may be part of the strand of a peacock's tail feathers (if it be a large fly, such as the drake or May fly); but if for a smaller fly you are making, then take some simple hair. The same materials will also answer for the horns of a fly, which latter of course you must tie down at the head. Fasten your gold or silver twist after the same manner; tie first at one end of the hook, and wind it round till you come to the other end of the bend, and then tie again. You must be careful to leave off at the opposite end of the hook with the silk you first of all whip it on with, to that end where you fasten your hackle, because you will in that case have silk to fasten down either your horns or tails at the proper place, without winding backwards and forwards, and thus encumbering your fly with too much silk. STUDY GREAT NEATNESS IN ALL YOUR WORK.

CHAPTER XII.

THAT IT DOES NOT REQUIRE DELICATE, TAPERING FINGERS TO MAKE FLIES—EXEMPLIFIED IN THE CASE OF A FIRST-RATE FLY-FISHER WHOSE HANDS AND FINGERS WERE REMARKABLY CLUMSY—FISHING WITH *LIVE* MAY-FLIES OR DRAKES CONDEMNED, BEING NOT ONLY CRUEL, BUT QUITE UNNECESSARY—HOW TO THROW YOUR LINES IN WINDY WEATHER AND AT ALL OTHER TIMES—WITH A FEW OBSERVATIONS IN CONCLUSION.

It has been said that women make better flies than men, their fingers being smaller and more tapering. This, however, I do not consider to be the cause, but their patience. Females again are in the habit of employing themselves in works of extreme neatness; hence they are more at home in making flies than men. Great practice in both sexes will produce equally good results. Many years ago I knew a man, a first-rate fisher and fly-maker, well known and of great celebrity, a native of Lancashire, I believe. He is said to have begun his fishing excursion regularly in the early spring, commencing in the West of England, fishing his way up to the Northern parts of the kingdom, thus frequenting various rivers at the proper seasons, as it is a well-known fact that rivers in general are available for fly-fishing earlier or later in the year in progression from west and south to north, even to the northern parts of Scotland. I had the good fortune to meet this experienced angler on his travels, staying with him at the same hotel, the Rutland Arms, in Bakewell, Derbyshire. I say the good fortune, because I became his pupil in fly-making. If this Mr. W——d had borrowed a pair of thumbs and a set of fingers from the clumsiest clodhopper in the agricultural world, they might still have been more delicate and tapering than his own; and yet this gentleman could make the smallest, neatest, and most beautiful flies. I do not recollect to have seen in the best fishing-tackle shops, whether in London or elsewhere, flies so small and delicate; so perfect a master was he of his art. If Newton could solve a problem, or Paganini execute a passage on the violin, so Mr. W——d could make a fly. I mention this instance to prove that no one need despair of making flies from want of delicate, tapering fingers. Before we dismiss this gentleman, it will be in accordance with the merciful object of this treatise to mention a circumstance which occurred in the neighbourhood of Bakewell,* on the banks of that far-famed brilliant stream (the brightest perhaps in England, it may be in the world) *the Latchkill*. It was on one of those days in direct opposition to that described in Walton and Cotton's "Angler"—

> "A day without too bright a beam,
> "A warm but not a scorching sun,
> "A southern breeze to curl the stream,
> "And, master, half our work is done."

For the day I am mentioning was one of the *brightest*; no breeze, and the river was like a looking-glass. On the banks of the above little stream, with rod and line, bending on one knee, nearly prostrate to prevent the fish from seeing him, imagine that you beheld this jolly angler (for such he was in many senses of the word) vainly endeavouring in the broiling sun to catch one single fish; though every now and then, I am sorry to say, he took out of his drake basket a *live* fly, which he spitted with his hook, and very gently throwing it on the water, using extreme

* Bakewell is situate on the river Wye, Derbyshire, in a beautiful and picturesque vale. The engraving is introduced, being the place of resort by many anglers, who, by the kind and condescending permission of the Duke of Rutland, have liberty to fish in the neighbouring trout streams, of which there are many, strictly preserved by his Grace for the amusement of the visitors at the Rutland Arms, in Bakewell, and at the Peacock Inn, Rowsley.

BAKEWELL.

care lest he should tear out the hook, and thus lose his fly, or that a sudden jerk might kill the insect, and prevent its fluttering on the water to entice the trout. During this merciless proceeding I ventured to approach him, and naturally observed, "Do you think, Sir, those insects feel at "all?" "Feel?" he replied, and at the same time suiting the action to the word, he passed the hook through the body of one of his victims, adding, "As much as any Christian." At that time I happened to have in my book one of those artificial Winchester May flies with the wing reversed, and immediately commenced fishing with it, to the disdain of my brother angler with his *live* flies, who looked upon me, I believe, after some such manner as Goliath eyed David. However, I persevered in the broad sun-light, and after a few casts I hooked a fish, and then another, to the astonishment of the old gentleman. And before I got home to the inn (notwithstanding the still air and scorching sun, and water of the colour and appearance of crystal), I had managed to secure a good dish of trout; and I had left the *live fly angler* with an empty pannier to pursue his reflections on the many living little creatures whom he had spitted alive to no purpose but to die a miserable death, either from drowning or the effects of the impalement by the hook, or from both.

I have related the above anecdote to prove that in every instance as much may be done with the *dead* bait, and perhaps much *more* than with the *live* one; for where will you find a stream so clear as the Latchkill, or the fish which inhabit it so shy?

If with an artificial fly, on a stream like that, you can exceed the sport of the most celebrated angler with his *live* flies, little doubt remains that on common streams, the waters of which are far less transparent, your advantage over him would be greater; why, then, should recourse be had to the live fly? Not to mention the cruelty, the sport is much deteriorated by the live principle—it partakes of the nature of *poaching*; whereas in fishing with an artificial fly (especially with one of your own making) you have the satisfaction of knowing that you are relying on your own resources, calling forth into action all the skill of the accomplished fly angler, not relying on the work of others, made ready to your hand, purchased at the shops, or given to you. The graceful flow of your line, behind, before, and around you, with its appended fly made to reach its destination with fairy fall on the smooth or rippled stream—all these contribute to give pleasure to this fascinating amusement; but on the contrary, you destroy at once all the satisfaction and delight associated with the graceful art of fly-fishing, hardening your heart to behold the agonizing flutter of the poor harmless insect, and become neither more nor less than a heartless common poacher. You not unoften mar your success in taking fish: should you catch them, you do not enjoy half the satisfaction in possessing them. Away then with the *live* fly, and leave him to enjoy his existence in the sunny ray. One day's existence is frequently his utmost limit: let him enjoy his short-lived nature, and cut him not off in the meridian sunshine of his day; open your drake basket and let him escape; and as he enjoys his liberty, ascending with majestic motion in the glorious sunlight, your relenting heart will experience an inward joy as you view his heavenward flight far greater than having made him the victim of your cruelty for securing your prey.

With a few observations on the best method of casting your line, I shall hasten to conclude.

Should you be fly-fishing on a windy day, you should be the more careful in noticing every direction I am about to give, or you will crack off many a fly, entangle your line in the trees and bushes, or even on your own person, especially if the wind should happen to be in your face, or at right angles.

In windy days do not be tempted to fish with too long a line; because, should the wind chance to be in your favour, that is behind you or nearly so, in that case you will be liable to whip off your fly: besides, the fish will not be so likely to see you when there is a strong ripple on the water; and as you may approach nearer to the bank, therefore you will not require so long a line. Be very careful, whether on quiet or stormy days, not to return your fly in the same wake when you are endeavouring to throw it; I mean, not like the passage of the thong of a hunting whip when you crack it. If you should do so, you will inevitably break off your fly. I know the difficulty of avoiding this when you are fishing among bushes or trees on the right and left of you. As a general rule, throw in a curve, letting the fly swing round you in a sufficient area, so as to avoid anything like a snap: when it shall have performed this revolution, you may send it forward with all your might, without the chance of losing it. This regularity of throwing, you must not expect to accomplish on a windy day: so make up your mind to sacrifice a fly or two on such occasions.

Endeavour to make your line in falling touch the water first at about three yards above the fly where the gut ought to begin, that the fly may skip over the remaining distance, and *gently* fall on the surface of the water, as the natural fly would fall. Avoid drawing it as much as you can, but let it *sail* down the stream as far as the length of the line will admit; then draw it towards you, but not *up* the current; *across* the water if possible, or diagonally if you cannot effect this; for the natural fly never swims up the stream. Some good fishermen use three or four flies: I prefer to employ one fly, a good end fly, of the season— many a good fish having been lost by the bob or side-flies catching on a weed or a root, and frequently on the landing net, thus preventing the play of the rod. The plan may be all very well when fishing for small fry, such as bleak, which you can pull out at once without requiring the aid of a landing net. Still, in the height of summer, when the weeds are prevalent, the plan is a bad one. You may catch, it is true, two or even three little fish at a time; but still you may lose many a "whopper" (as anglers style the heavier fish) by your superfluous flies coming in contact with roots or weeds. Look well to the joinings of your gut, and do not trust to those, generally made with waxed silk, which you buy at the shops. Cut out all those fastenings, and join the gut again with a fisherman's knot, made on the following principle: at the extremity of one of the lengths affect to tie a knot, but proceed no further than to make the little circle previously to tying it closely: in this small round hole insert the end of another length, and draw it a little way up the first length and tie it on the same; then tie down the first knot where you left the little circle and draw the two knots together; cut off the superfluous gut at the end of each knot and the joining is complete, much neater and vastly stronger than the wax and silk fastening plan. Besides, if you will fish with a bob-fly, you can insert him with his gut about four inches long and with a little knot at the end before you draw the two knots together, as above directed, in the space left between the knots, instead of the clumsy plan of putting the bob-fly on with a sliding noose.

When you have a rise, strike with a sudden but gentle jerk, and never slacken your line afterwards till you shall have landed your fish. Keep him as near to the surface as you well can till you shall have tired him out; otherwise he may get into the weeds, or by the sides of large stones, at the bottom; and moreover, he will have less power to pull against you the nearer you keep him to the top of the water.

As a farewell address to my readers I would impress on all the brotherhood of the angle once more the necessity of never losing sight of mercy in following the then harmless amusement of angling in order to a true and unmingled enjoyment of the pursuit. A fish, unless it be the eel, is soon and easily killed on being caught; and then its pain and misery are at an end. The live bait, as I have endeavoured to show (from facts and experience), need never be used. The captured fish need suffer only a small and short infliction of pain, if killed IMMEDIATELY ON BEING TAKEN.

By a thorough knowledge and practice of the foregoing rules, how much will your recreation be enhanced! With what satisfaction and pleasure will you enter on your fishing day! No self-accusing thoughts at night of wanton cruelty, shown to harmless fish, worms, and insects. The recollection of your mercy in avoiding, by every possible care, to inflict pain on your captured victims, will give a zest to your anticipation of another day's fishing, with its general accompaniments of balmy air, refreshing breeze, to contemplate the works of God, in Nature's lovely scenes,

CONCLUSION.

beside the bubbling current or tranquil stream. And in those solitudes which anglers love to frequent, in the calm eventide, when sombre twilight begins to draw on; after a delightful day's recreation, the mind of the contemplative Christian will, in imagination, visit the mountain scenery of Galilee's blue dark waters, where the early training of Apostles began in calling forth enterprise, patience, caution, and hardy endurance, and joining in mind the honoured guests of the blessed Redeemer at their primitive and frugal and sweet repast of "broiled fish and honeycomb," and thus learn lessons of love and admiration towards the Master, and love towards mankind, with hopes inspired for all who love and serve Him to join the goodly company of merciful fishermen, assembled at the table of His goodness, in His own blessed country.

[JANUARY 1868.]

GENERAL LIST OF WORKS

PUBLISHED BY

MESSRS. LONGMANS, GREEN, AND CO.

PATERNOSTER ROW, LONDON.

Historical Works.

LORD MACAULAY'S WORKS. Complete and Uniform Library Edition. Edited by his Sister, Lady TREVELYAN. 8 vols. 8vo. with Portrait, price £5 5s. cloth, or £3 8s. bound in tree-calf by Rivière.

The **HISTORY of ENGLAND** from the Fall of Wolsey to the Death of Elizabeth. By JAMES ANTHONY FROUDE, M.A. late Fellow of Exeter College, Oxford. VOLS. 1. to X. in 8vo. price £7 2s. cloth.

VOLS. I. to IV. the Reign of Henry VIII. Third Edition, 54s.

VOLS. V. and VI. the Reigns of Edward VI. and Mary. Third Edition, 28s.

VOLS. VII. and VIII. the Reign of Elizabeth, VOLS. I. and II. Fourth Edition, 28s.

VOLS. IX. and X. the Reign of Elizabeth, VOLS. III. and IV. 32s.

The **HISTORY of ENGLAND** from the Accession of James II. By Lord MACAULAY.

LIBRARY EDITION, 5 vols. 8vo. £4.

CABINET EDITION, 8 vols. post 8vo. 48s.

PEOPLE'S EDITION, 4 vols. crown 8vo. 16s.

REVOLUTIONS in ENGLISH HISTORY. By ROBERT VAUGHAN, D.D. 3 vols. 8vo. 30s.

The **GOVERNMENT of ENGLAND**: its Structure and its Development. By WILLIAM EDWARD HEARN, LL.D. Professor of History and Political Economy in the University of Melbourne. 8vo. 14s.

PLUTOLOGY; or, the Theory of the Efforts to Satisfy Human Wants. By the same Author. 8vo. 14s.

An **ESSAY on the HISTORY of the ENGLISH GOVERNMENT** and Constitution, from the Reign of Henry VII. to the Present Time. By JOHN EARL RUSSELL. Fourth Edition, revised. Crown 8vo. 6s.

On **PARLIAMENTARY GOVERNMENT in ENGLAND**: Its Origin, Development, and Practical Operation. By ALPHEUS TODD, Librarian of the Legislative Assembly of Canada. In Two Volumes. VOL. I. 8vo. 16s.

A

The **HISTORY of ENGLAND** during the Reign of George the Third. By the Right Hon. W. N. MASSEY. Cabinet Edition. 4 vols. post 8vo. 24s.

The **CONSTITUTIONAL HISTORY of ENGLAND**, since the Accession of George III. 1760—1860. By Sir THOMAS ERSKINE MAY, C.B. Second Edition. 2 vols. 8vo. 33s.

CONSTITUTIONAL HISTORY of the BRITISH EMPIRE from the Accession of Charles I. to the Restoration. By G. BRODIE, Esq. Historiographer-Royal of Scotland. Second Edition. 3 vols. 8vo. 36s.

HISTORICAL STUDIES. By HENRY MERIVALE, M.A. 8vo. price 12. 6d.

The **OXFORD REFORMERS of 1498**; being a History of the Fellowwork of John Colet, Erasmus, and Thomas More. By FREDERIC SEEBOHM. 8vo. 12s.

LECTURES on the HISTORY of ENGLAND. By WILLIAM LONGMAN. VOL. I. from the Earliest Times to the Death of King Edward II. with 6 Maps, a coloured Plate, and 53 Woodcuts. 8vo. 15s.

HISTORY of CIVILISATION in England and France, Spain and Scotland. By HENRY THOMAS BUCKLE. Fifth Edition of the entire Work, with a complete INDEX. 3 vols. crown 8vo. 24s.

DEMOCRACY in AMERICA. By ALEXIS DE TOCQUEVILLE. Translated by HENRY REEVE, with an Introductory Notice by the Translator. 2 vols. 8vo. 21s.

The **SPANISH CONQUEST in AMERICA**, and its Relation to the History of Slavery and to the Government of Colonies. By ARTHUR HELPS. 4 vols. 8vo. £3. VOLS. I. and II. 28s. VOLS. III. and IV. 16s. each.

HISTORY of the REFORMATION in EUROPE in the Time of Calvin. By J. H. MERLE D'AUBIGNÉ, D.D. VOLS. I. and II. 8vo. 28s. and VOL. III. 12s. VOL. IV. 16s.

LIBRARY HISTORY of FRANCE, a New Work, complete in FIVE VOLUMES. By EYRE EVANS CROWE. VOL. I. 14s. VOL. II. 15s. VOL. III. 18s. VOL. IV. 18s.—VOL. V. *just ready*.

LECTURES on the HISTORY of FRANCE. By the late Sir JAMES STEPHEN, LL.D. 2 vols. 8vo. 24s.

The **HISTORY of GREECE.** By C. THIRLWALL, D.D. Lord Bishop of St. David's. 8 vols. fcp. 8vo. price 28s.

The **TALE of the GREAT PERSIAN WAR**, from the Histories of Herodotus. By GEORGE W. COX, M.A. Fcp. 7s. 6d.

GREEK HISTORY from Themistocles to Alexander, in a Series of Lives from Plutarch. Revised and arranged by A. H. CLOUGH. Fcp. with 44 Woodcuts, 6s.

CRITICAL HISTORY of the LANGUAGE and LITERATURE of Ancient Greece. By WILLIAM MURE, of Caldwell. 5 vols. 8vo. £3 9s.

HISTORY of the LITERATURE of ANCIENT GREECE. By Professor K. O. MÜLLER. Translated by the Right Hon. Sir GEORGE CORNEWALL LEWIS, Bart. and by J. W. DONALDSON, D.D. 3 vols. 8vo. 36s.

HISTORY of the CITY of ROME from its Foundation to the Sixteenth Century of the Christian Era. By THOMAS H. DYER, LL.D. 8vo. with 2 Maps, 15s.

HISTORY of the ROMANS under the EMPIRE. By the Rev. C. MERIVALE, LL.D. 8 vols. post 8vo. 48s.

The FALL of the ROMAN REPUBLIC: a Short History of the Last Century of the Commonwealth. By the same Author. 12mo. 7s. 6d.

The HISTORY of INDIA, from the Earliest Period to the close of Lord Dalhousie's Administration. By JOHN CLARK MARSHMAN. 3 vols. crown 8vo. 22s. 6d.

HISTORY of the FRENCH in INDIA, from the Founding of Pondichery in 1674 to its Capture in 1761. By Major G. B. MALLESON, Bengal Staff Corps. 8vo. 16s.

CRITICAL and HISTORICAL ESSAYS contributed to the *Edinburgh Review*. By the Right Hon. LORD MACAULAY.

LIBRARY EDITION, 3 vols. 8vo. 36s.
CABINET EDITION, 4 vols. post 8vo. 24s.
TRAVELLER'S EDITION, in One Volume, square crown 8vo. 21s.
POCKET EDITION, 3 vols. fcp. 21s.
PEOPLE'S EDITION, 2 vols. crown 8vo. 8s.

The PAPAL DRAMA: an Historical Essay, wherein the Story of the Popedom of Rome is narrated from its Origin to the Present Time. By THOMAS H. GILL. 8vo. 12s.

GOD in HISTORY; or, the Progress of Man's Faith in a Moral Order of the World. By the late Baron BUNSEN. Translated from the German by SUSANNA WINKWORTH; with a Preface by ARTHUR PENRHYN STANLEY, D.D. Dean of Westminster. VOLS. I. and II. 8vo. [*Nearly ready.*

HISTORY of the RISE and INFLUENCE of the SPIRIT of RATIONALISM in EUROPE. By W. E. H. LECKY, M.A. Third Edition, revised. 2 vols. 8vo. 25s.

The HISTORY of PHILOSOPHY, from Thales to Comte. By GEORGE HENRY LEWES. Third Edition. 2 vols. 8vo. 30s.

EGYPT'S PLACE in UNIVERSAL HISTORY; an Historical Investigation. By Baron BUNSEN, D.C.L. Translated by C. H. COTTRELL, M.A. With Additions by S. BIRCH, LL.D. VOL. I. New Edition, revised and enlarged, price 31s. 6d. VOLS. II. 30s. VOLS. III. and IV. 25s. each; VOL. V. just published, 63s. The Set complete, in 5 vols. 8vo. price £8 14s. 6d.

MAUNDER'S HISTORICAL TREASURY; comprising a General Introductory Outline of Universal History, and a series of Separate Histories. Fcp. 10s.

HISTORY of the CHRISTIAN CHURCH, from the Ascension of Christ to the Conversion of Constantine. By E. BURTON, D.D. late Prof. of Divinity in the Univ. of Oxford. Eighth Edition. Fcp. 3s. 6d.

SKETCH of the HISTORY of the CHURCH of ENGLAND to the Revolution of 1688. By the Right Rev. T. V. SHORT, D.D. Lord Bishop of St. Asaph. Seventh Edition. Crown 8vo. 10s. 6d.

HISTORY of the EARLY CHURCH, from the First Preaching of the Gospel to the Council of Nicæa, A.D. 325. By ELIZABETH M. SEWELL, Author of 'Amy Herbert.' Fcp. 4s. 6d.

The **ENGLISH REFORMATION.** By F. C. MASSINGBERD, M.A. Chancellor of Lincoln and Rector of South Ormsby. Fourth Edition, revised. Fcp. 8vo. 7s. 6d.

HISTORY of WESLEYAN METHODISM. By GEORGE SMITH, F.A.S. Fourth Edition, with numerous Portraits. 3 vols. cr. 8vo. 7s. each.

Biography and Memoirs.

DICTIONARY of GENERAL BIOGRAPHY; containing Concise Memoirs and Notices of the most Eminent Persons of all Countries, from the Earliest Ages to the Present Time. Edited by W. L. R. CATES. 8vo. 21s.

MEMOIRS of Sir PHILIP FRANCIS, K.C.B. with Correspondence and Journals. Commenced by the late JOSEPH PARKES; completed and edited by HERMAN MERIVALE, M.A. 2 vols. 8vo. with Portrait and Facsimiles, 30s.

LIFE of BARON BUNSEN. By Baroness BUNSEN. Drawn chiefly from Family Papers. With Two Portraits taken at different periods of the Baron's life, and several Lithographic Views. 2 vols. 8vo. [*Nearly ready.*

LIFE and CORRESPONDENCE of RICHARD WHATELY, D.D. late Archbishop of Dublin. By E. JANE WHATELY, Author of 'English Synonymes.' With Two Portraits. 2 vols. 8vo. 28s.

EXTRACTS of the JOURNALS and CORRESPONDENCE of MISS BERRY, from the Year 1783 to 1852. Edited by Lady THERESA LEWIS. Second Edition, with 3 Portraits. 3 vols. 8vo. 42s.

LIFE of the DUKE of WELLINGTON. By the Rev. G. R. GLEIG, M.A. Popular Edition, carefully revised; with copious Additions. Crown 8vo. with Portrait, 5s.

HISTORY of MY RELIGIOUS OPINIONS. By J. H. NEWMAN, D.D. Being the Substance of Apologia pro Vitâ Suâ. Post 8vo. 6s.

FATHER MATHEW: a Biography. By JOHN FRANCIS MAGUIRE, M.P. for Cork. Popular Edition, with Portrait. Crown 8vo. 3s. 6d.

Rome; its Rulers and its Institutions. By the same Author. New Edition nearly ready.

LETTERS of DISTINGUISHED MUSICIANS, viz. Gluck, Haydn, P. E. Bach, Weber, and Mendelssohn. Translated from the German by Lady WALLACE. With Three Portraits. Post 8vo. 14s.

FELIX MENDELSSOHN'S LETTERS from *Italy and Switzerland*, and *Letters from* 1833 *to* 1847, translated by Lady WALLACE. New Edition, with Portrait. 2 vols. crown 8vo. 5s. each.

MOZART'S LETTERS (1769–1791), translated from the Collection of Dr. LUDWIG NOHL by Lady WALLACE. 2 vols. post 8vo. with Portrait and Facsimile, 18s.

BEETHOVEN'S LETTERS (1790–1826), Translated from the Collection of Dr. NOHL by Lady WALLACE. 2 vols. post 8vo. with Portrait, 18s.

FARADAY as a DISCOVERER: a Memoir. By JOHN TYNDALL, LL.D. F.R.S. Professor of Natural Philosophy in the Royal Institution of Great Britain, and in the Royal School of Mines. Crown 8vo. [*Nearly ready.*

MEMOIRS of SIR HENRY HAVELOCK, K.C.B. By JOHN CLARK MARSHMAN. Cabinet Edition, with Portrait. Crown 8vo. price 5s.

LIFE of PASTOR FLIEDNER, Founder of the Deaconesses' Institution at Kaiserswerth. Translated from the German by CATHERINE WINKWORTH. Fcp. 8vo. with Portrait, 3s. 6d.

LIFE of FRANZ SCHUBERT, translated from the German of KEITZLE VON HELLBORN by ARTHUR DUKE COLERIDGE, M.A. late Fellow of King's College, Cambridge. [*Nearly ready.*

WITH MAXIMILIAN in MEXICO. From the Note-Book of a Mexican Officer. By MAX. Baron VON ALVENSLEBEN, late Lieutenant in the Imperial Mexican Army. Post 8vo. 7s. 6d.

VICISSITUDES of FAMILIES. By Sir BERNARD BURKE, Ulster King of Arms. FIRST, SECOND, and THIRD SERIES. 3 vols. crown 8vo. 12s. 6d. each.

ESSAYS in ECCLESIASTICAL BIOGRAPHY. By the Right Hon. Sir J. STEPHEN, LL.D. Cabinet Edition (being the Fifth). Crown 8vo. 7s. 6d.

MAUNDER'S BIOGRAPHICAL TREASURY. Thirteenth Edition, reconstructed, thoroughly revised, and in great part rewritten; with about 1,000 additional Memoirs and Notices, by W. L. R. CATES. Fcp. 10s. 6d.

LETTERS and LIFE of FRANCIS BACON, including all his Occasional Works. Collected and edited, with a Commentary, by J. SPEDDING, Trin. Coll. Cantab. VOLS. I. and II. 8vo. 24s.

Criticism, Philosophy, Polity, &c.

The **INSTITUTES of JUSTINIAN**; with English Introduction, Translation, and Notes. By T. C. SANDARS, M.A. Barrister, late Fellow of Oriel Coll. Oxon. Third Edition. 8vo. 15s.

The **ETHICS of ARISTOTLE**, illustrated with Essays and Notes. By Sir A. GRANT, Bart. M.A. LL.D. Second Edition, revised and completed. 2 vols. 8vo. price 28s.

ELEMENTS of LOGIC. By R. WHATELY, D.D. late Archbishop of Dublin. Ninth Edition. 8vo. 10s. 6d. crown 8vo. 4s. 6d.

Elements of Rhetoric. By the same Author. Seventh Edition. 8vo. 10s. 6d. crown 8vo. 4s. 6d.

English Synonymes. Edited by Archbishop WHATELY. 5th Edition. Fcp. 3s.

BACON'S ESSAYS with ANNOTATIONS. By R. WHATELY, D.D. late Archbishop of Dublin. Sixth Edition. 8vo. 10s. 6d.

LORD BACON'S WORKS, collected and edited by R. L. ELLIS, M.A. J. SPEDDING, M.A. and D. D. HEATH. Vols. I. to V. *Philosophical Works,* 5 vols. 8vo. £4 6s. VOLS. VI. and VII. *Literary and Professional Works,* 2 vols. £1 16s.

On **REPRESENTATIVE GOVERNMENT.** By JOHN STUART MILL, M.P. for Westminster. Third Edition, 8vo. 9s. crown 8vo. 2s.

On **LIBERTY.** By JOHN STUART MILL, M.P. for Westminster. Third Edition. Post 8vo. 7s. 6d. crown 8vo. 1s. 4d.

Principles of Political Economy. By the same Author. Sixth Edition. 2 vols. 8vo. 30s. or in 1 vol. crown 8vo. 5s.

A System of Logic, Ratiocinative and Inductive. By the same Author. Sixth Edition. Two vols. 8vo. 25s.

Utilitarianism. By the same Author. Second Edition. 8vo. 5s.

Dissertations and Discussions, Political, Philosophical, and Historical. By the same Author. Second Edition, revised. 3 vols. 8vo. 36s.

Examination of Sir W. Hamilton's Philosophy, and of the Principal Philosophical Questions discussed in his Writings. By the same Author. Third Edition. 8vo. 16s.

WORKMEN and WAGES at HOME and ABROAD; or, the Effects of Strikes, Combinations, and Trade Unions. By J. WARD, Author of 'The World in its Workshops,' &c. Post 8vo. 7s. 6d.

The ELEMENTS of POLITICAL ECONOMY. By HENRY DUNNING MACLEOD, M.A. Barrister-at-Law. 8vo. 16s.

A Dictionary of Political Economy; Biographical, Bibliographical, Historical, and Practical. By the same Author. VOL. I. royal 8vo. 30s.

An OUTLINE of the NECESSARY LAWS of THOUGHT: a Treatise on Pure and Applied Logic. By the Most Rev. W. THOMSON, D.D. Archbishop of York. Crown 8vo. 5s. 6d.

ANALYSIS of Mr. MILL'S SYSTEM of LOGIC. By W. STEBBING, M.A. Fellow of Worcester College, Oxford. Second Edition. 12mo. 3s. 6d.

The ELECTION of REPRESENTATIVES, Parliamentary and Municipal; a Treatise. By THOMAS HARE, Barrister-at-Law. Third Edition, with Additions. Crown 8vo. 6s.

SPEECHES of the RIGHT HON. LORD MACAULAY, corrected by Himself. Library Edition, 8vo. 12s. People's Edition, crown 8vo. 3s. 6d.

LORD MACAULAY'S SPEECHES on PARLIAMENTARY REFORM in 1831 and 1832. 16mo. 1s.

SPEECHES on PARLIAMENTARY REFORM, delivered in the House of Commons by the Right Hon. B. DISRAELI (1848-1866). Edited by MONTAGU CORRY, B.A. Second Edition. 8vo. 12s.

INAUGURAL ADDRESS delivered to the University of St. Andrews. By JOHN STUART MILL. 8vo. 5s. People's Edition, crown 8vo. 1s.

A DICTIONARY of the ENGLISH LANGUAGE. By R. G. LATHAM, M.A. M.D. F.R.S. Founded on the Dictionary of Dr. S. JOHNSON, as edited by the Rev. H. J. TODD, with numerous Emendations and Additions. In Two Volumes. VOL. I. 4to. in Two Parts, price £3 10s. In course of publication, also, in 36 Parts, price 3s. 6d. each.

THESAURUS of ENGLISH WORDS and PHRASES, classified and arranged so as to facilitate the Expression of Ideas, and assist in Literary Composition. By P. M. ROGET, M.D. New Edition. Crown 8vo. 10s. 6d.

LECTURES on the SCIENCE of LANGUAGE, delivered at the Royal Institution. By MAX MÜLLER, M.A. Taylorian Professor in the University of Oxford. FIRST SERIES, Fifth Edition, 12s. SECOND SERIES, 18s.

CHAPTERS on LANGUAGE. By FREDERIC W. FARRAR, F.R.S. late Fellow of Trin. Coll. Cambridge. Crown 8vo. 8s. 6d.

The DEBATER; a Series of Complete Debates, Outlines of Debates, and Questions for Discussion. By F. ROWTON. Fcp. 6s.

A COURSE of ENGLISH READING, adapted to every taste and capacity; or, How and What to Read. By the Rev. J. PYCROFT, B.A. Fourth Edition. Fcp. 5s.

MANUAL of ENGLISH LITERATURE, Historical and Critical. By THOMAS ARNOLD, M.A. Second Edition. Crown 8vo. price 7s. 6d.

SOUTHEY'S DOCTOR, complete in One Volume. Edited by the Rev. J. W. WARTER, B.D. Square crown 8vo. 12s. 6d.

HISTORICAL and CRITICAL COMMENTARY on the OLD TESTAMENT; with a New Translation. By M. M. KALISCH, Ph.D. VOL. I. Genesis, 8vo. 18s. or adapted for the General Reader, 12s. VOL. II. Exodus, 15s. or adapted for the General Reader, 12s. VOL. III. Leviticus, PART I. 15s. or adapted for the General Reader, 8s.

A Hebrew Grammar, with Exercises. By the same Author. PART I. Outlines with Exercises, 8vo. 12s. 6d. KEY, 5s. PART II. Exceptional Forms and Constructions, 12s. 6d.

A LATIN-ENGLISH DICTIONARY. By J. T. WHITE, D.D. of Corpus Christi College, and J. E. RIDDLE, M.A. of St. Edmund Hall, Oxford. Imperial 8vo. pp. 2,128, price 42s. cloth.

A New Latin-English Dictionary, abridged from the larger work of White and Riddle (as above), by J. T. WHITE, D.D. Joint-Author. Medium 8vo. pp. 1,048, price 18s. cloth.

The Junior Scholar's Latin-English Dictionary, abridged from the larger works of White and Riddle (as above), by J. T. White, D.D. surviving Joint-Author. Square 12mo. pp. 662, price 7s. 6d. cloth.

An ENGLISH-GREEK LEXICON, containing all the Greek Words used by Writers of good authority. By C. D. YONGE, B.A. Fifth Edition. 4to. 21s.

Mr. YONGE'S NEW LEXICON, English and Greek, abridged from his larger work (as above). Revised Edition. Square 12mo. 8s. 6d.

A GREEK-ENGLISH LEXICON. Compiled by H. G. LIDDELL, D.D. Dean of Christ Church, and R. SCOTT, D.D. Master of Balliol. Fifth Edition. Crown 4to. 31s. 6d.

A Lexicon, Greek and English, abridged from LIDDELL and SCOTT's Greek-English Lexicon. Eleventh Edition. Square 12mo. 7s. 6d.

A SANSKRIT-ENGLISH DICTIONARY, the Sanskrit words printed both in the original Devanagari and in Roman letters. Compiled by T. BENFEY, Prof. in the Univ. of Göttingen. 8vo. 52s. 6d.

A PRACTICAL DICTIONARY of the FRENCH and ENGLISH LANGUAGES. By L. CONTANSEAU. Thirteenth Edition. Post 8vo. 10s. 6d.

Contanseau's Pocket Dictionary, French and English, abridged from the above by the Author. New and Cheaper Edition, 18mo. 3s. 6d.

NEW PRACTICAL DICTIONARY of the GERMAN LANGUAGE; German-English and English-German. By the Rev. W. L. BLACKLEY, M.A. and Dr. CARL MARTIN FRIEDLÄNDER. Cheaper Issue, post 8vo. 7s. 6d.

Miscellaneous Works and *Popular Metaphysics.*

LESSONS of MIDDLE AGE, with some Account of various Cities and Men. By A. K. H. B. Author of 'The Recreations of a Country Parson.' Post 8vo. 9s.

RECREATIONS of a COUNTRY PARSON. By A. K. H. B. A New and carefully revised Edition of the SECOND SERIES. Crown 8vo. 3s. 6d.

The Common-place Philosopher in Town and Country. By the same Author. Crown 8vo. 3s. 6d.

Leisure Hours in Town; Essays Consolatory, Æsthetical, Moral, Social, and Domestic. By the same Author. Crown 8vo. 3s. 6d.

The Autumn Holidays of a Country Parson; Essays contributed to *Fraser's Magazine* and to *Good Words.* By the same. Crown 8vo. 3s. 6d.

The Graver Thoughts of a Country Parson. SECOND SERIES. By the same Author. Crown 8vo. 3s. 6d.

Critical Essays of a Country Parson. Selected from Essays contributed to *Fraser's Magazine.* By the same Author. Crown 8vo. 3s. 6d.

Sunday Afternoons at the Parish Church of a Scottish University City. By the same Author. Crown 8vo. 3s. 6d.

SHORT STUDIES on GREAT SUBJECTS. By JAMES ANTHONY FROUDE, M.A. late Fellow of Exeter Coll. Oxford. Second Edition. 8vo. 12s.

STUDIES in PARLIAMENT. A Series of Sketches of Leading Politicians. By R. H. HUTTON. Crown 8vo. 4s. 6d.

LORD MACAULAY'S MISCELLANEOUS WRITINGS.
> LIBRARY EDITION. 2 vols. 8vo. Portrait, 21s.
> PEOPLE'S EDITION. 1 vol. crown 8vo. 4s. 6d.

The REV. SYDNEY SMITH'S MISCELLANEOUS WORKS; including his Contributions to the *Edinburgh Review.* 2 vols. crown 8vo. 8s.

Elementary Sketches of Moral Philosophy, delivered at the Royal Institution. By the Rev. SYDNEY SMITH, M.A. Fourth Edition. Fcp. 6s.

The Wit and Wisdom of the Rev. Sydney Smith: a Selection of the most memorable Passages in his Writings and Conversation. 16mo. 5s.

EPIGRAMS, Ancient and Modern; Humorous, Witty, Satirical, Moral, and Panegyrical. Edited by Rev. JOHN BOOTH, B.A. Cambridge. Second Edition, revised and enlarged. Fcp. 7s. 6d.

From MATTER to SPIRIT: the Result of Ten Years' Experience in Spirit Manifestations. By SOPHIA E. DE MORGAN. With a PREFACE by her Husband, Professor DE MORGAN. Post 8vo. 8s. 6d.

The PEDIGREE of the ENGLISH PEOPLE; an Argument, Historical and Scientific, on the *Ethnology* of the English. By THOMAS NICHOLAS, M.A. Ph.D. 8vo. 16s.

The ENGLISH and THEIR ORIGIN: a Prologue to authentic English History. By LUKE OWEN PIKE, M.A. Barrister-at-Law. 8vo. 9s.

ESSAYS selected from CONTRIBUTIONS to the *Edinburgh Review.* By HENRY ROGERS. Second Edition. 3 vols. fcp. 21s.

Reason and Faith, their Claims and Conflicts. By the same Author. New Edition, accompanied by several other Essays. Crown 8vo. 6s. 6d.

The Eclipse of Faith; or, a Visit to a Religious Sceptic. By the same Author. Eleventh Edition. Fcp. 5s.

Defence of the Eclipse of Faith, by its Author; a rejoinder to Dr. Newman's *Reply.* Third Edition. Fcp. 3s. 6d.

Selections from the Correspondence of R. E. H. Greyson. By the same Author. Third Edition. Crown 8vo. 7s. 6d.

OCCASIONAL ESSAYS. By CHANDOS WREN HOSKYNS, Author of 'Talpa, or the Chronicles of a Clay Farm,' &c. 16mo. 5s. 6d.

CHIPS from a GERMAN WORKSHOP; being Essays on the Science of Religion, and on Mythology, Traditions, and Customs. By MAX MÜLLER, M.A. Fellow of All Souls College, Oxford. 2 vols. 8vo. 21s.

An INTRODUCTION to MENTAL PHILOSOPHY, on the Inductive Method. By. J. D. MORELL, M.A. LL.D. 8vo. 12s.

Elements of Psychology, containing the Analysis of the Intellectual Powers. By the same Author. Post 8vo. 7s. 6d.

The SECRET of HEGEL: being the Hegelian System in Origin, Principle, Form, and Matter. By J. H. STIRLING. 2 vols. 8vo. 28s.

The SENSES and the INTELLECT. By ALEXANDER BAIN, M.A. Professor of Logic in the University of Aberdeen. Second Edition. 8vo. 15s.

The EMOTIONS and the WILL. By ALEXANDER BAIN, M.A. Professor of Logic in the University of Aberdeen. Second Edition. 8vo. 15s.

On the Study of Character, including an Estimate of Phrenology. By the same Author. 8vo. 9s.

TIME and SPACE: a Metaphysical Essay. By SHADWORTH H. HODGSON. 8vo. price 16s.

B

CHRISTIAN SCHOOLS and SCHOLARS; or, Sketches of Education from the Christian Era to the Council of Trent. By the Author of 'The Three Chancellors,' &c. 2 vols. 8vo. 30s.

The WAY to REST: Results from a Life-search after Religious Truth. By R. Vaughan, D.D. Crown 8vo. 7s. 6d.

The PHILOSOPHY of NECESSITY; or, Natural Law as applicable to Mental, Moral, and Social Science. By Charles Bray. Second Edition. 8vo. 9s.

The Education of the Feelings and Affections. By the same Author. Third Edition. 8vo. 3s. 6d.

On Force, its Mental and Moral Correlates. By the same Author. 8vo. 5s.

The FOLK-LORE of the NORTHERN COUNTIES of ENGLAND and the Borders. By William Henderson. With an Appendix on Household Stories by the Rev. S. Baring-Gould, M.A. Post 8vo. 9s. 6d.

Astronomy, Meteorology, Popular Geography, &c.

OUTLINES of ASTRONOMY. By Sir J. F. W. Herschel, Bart. M.A. Ninth Edition, revised; with Plates and Woodcuts. 8vo. 18s.

SATURN and its SYSTEM. By Richard A. Proctor, B.A. late Scholar of St John's Coll. Camb. 8vo. with 14 Plates, 14s.

Handbook of the Stars. By the same Author. With 3 Maps. Square fcp. 5s.

CELESTIAL OBJECTS for COMMON TELESCOPES. By the Rev. T. W. Webb, M.A. F.R.A.S. Revised Edition. [*Nearly ready.*

DOVE'S LAW of STORMS, considered in connection with the Ordinary Movements of the Atmosphere. Translated by R. H. Scott, M.A. T.C.D. 8vo. 10s. 6d.

PHYSICAL GEOGRAPHY for SCHOOLS and GENERAL READERS. By M. F. Maury, LL.D. Fcp. with 2 Charts, 2s. 6d.

M'CULLOCH'S DICTIONARY, Geographical, Statistical, and Historical, of the various Countries, Places, and Principal Natural Objects in the World. New Edition, with the Statistical Information brought up to the latest returns by F. Martin. 4 vols. 8vo. with coloured Maps, £4 4s.

A GENERAL DICTIONARY of GEOGRAPHY, Descriptive, Physical, Statistical, and Historical: forming a complete Gazetteer of the World. By A. Keith Johnston, LL.D. F.R.G.S. Revised to July 1867. 8vo. 31s. 6d.

A MANUAL of GEOGRAPHY, Physical, Industrial, and Political. By W. Hughes, F.R.G.S. With 6 Maps. Fcp. 7s. 6d.

The STATES of the RIVER PLATE: their Industries and Commerce. By Wilfrid Latham, Buenos Ayres. Second Edition, revised. 8vo. 12s.

HAWAII; the Past, Present, and Future of its Island-Kingdom: an Historical Account of the Sandwich Islands. By MANLEY HOPKINS, Second Edition, with Portrait, Map, &c. Post 8vo. 12s. 6d.

MAUNDER'S TREASURY of GEOGRAPHY, Physical, Historical, Descriptive, and Political. Edited by W. HUGHES, F.R.G.S. With 7 Maps and 16 Plates. Fcp. 10s. 6d.

Natural History and *Popular Science.*

ELEMENTARY TREATISE on PHYSICS, Experimental and Applied. Translated and edited from GANOT'S *Eléments de Physique* (with the Author's sanction) by E. ATKINSON, Ph. D. F.C.S. New Edition, revised and enlarged; with a Coloured Plate and 620 Woodcuts. Post 8vo. 15s.

The ELEMENTS of PHYSICS or NATURAL PHILOSOPHY. By NEIL ARNOTT, M.D. F.R.S. Physician Extraordinary to the Queen. Sixth Edition, rewritten and completed. Two Parts, 8vo. 21s.

SOUND: a Course of Eight Lectures delivered at the Royal Institution of Great Britain. By JOHN TYNDALL, LL.D. F.R.S. Crown 8vo. with Portrait of *M. Chladni* and 169 Woodcuts, price 9s.

HEAT CONSIDERED as a MODE of MOTION. By Professor JOHN TYNDALL, LL.D. F.R.S. Third Edition. Crown 8vo. with Woodcuts, 10s. 6d.

LIGHT: Its Influence on Life and Health. By FORBES WINSLOW, M.D. D.C.L. Oxon. (Hon.). Fcp. 8vo. 6s.

An ESSAY on DEW, and several Appearances connected with it. By W. C. WELLS. Edited, with Annotations, by L. P. CASELLA, F.R.A.S. and an Appendix by R. STRACHAN, F.M.S. 8vo. 5s.

ROCKS CLASSIFIED and DESCRIBED. By BERNHARD VON COTTA. An English Edition, by P. H. LAWRENCE (with English, German, and French Synonymes), revised by the Author. Post 8vo. 14s.

A TREATISE on ELECTRICITY, in Theory and Practice. By A. DE LA RIVE, Prof. in the Academy of Geneva. Translated by C. V. WALKER, F.R.S. 3 vols. 8vo. with Woodcuts, £3 13s.

The CORRELATION of PHYSICAL FORCES. By W. R. GROVE, Q.C. V.P.R.S. Fifth Edition, revised, and followed by a Discourse on Continuity. 8vo. 10s. 6d. The *Discourse on Continuity,* separately, 2s. 6d.

MANUAL of GEOLOGY. By S. HAUGHTON, M.D. F.R.S. Revised Edition, with 66 Woodcuts. Fcp. 7s. 6d.

A GUIDE to GEOLOGY. By J. PHILLIPS, M.A. Professor of Geology in the University of Oxford. Fifth Edition, with Plates. Fcp. 4s.

A GLOSSARY of MINERALOGY. By H. W. BRISTOW, F.G.S. of the Geological Survey of Great Britain. With 486 Figures. Crown 8vo. 6s.

VAN DER HOEVEN'S HANDBOOK of ZOOLOGY. Translated from the Second Dutch Edition by the Rev. W. CLARK, M.D. F.R.S. 2 vols. 8vo. with 24 Plates of Figures, 60s.

Professor **OWEN'S LECTURES** on the **COMPARATIVE ANATOMY** and Physiology of the Invertebrate Animals. Second Edition, with 235 Woodcuts. 8vo. 21s.

The **COMPARATIVE ANATOMY** and **PHYSIOLOGY** of the **VERTE**brate Animals. By RICHARD OWEN, F.R.S. D.C.L. 3 vols. 8vo. with above 1,200 Woodcuts. VOLS. I. and II. price 21s. each. VOL. III. just ready.

The **FIRST MAN** and **HIS PLACE** in **CREATION**, considered on the Principles of Common Sense from a Christian Point of View. By GEORGE MOORE, M.D. Post 8vo. 8s. 6d.

The **PRIMITIVE INHABITANTS** of **SCANDINAVIA**: an Essay on Comparative Ethnography, and a Contribution to the History of the Development of Mankind. Containing a description of the Implements, Dwellings, Tombs, and Mode of Living of the Savages in the North of Europe during the Stone Age. By SVEN NILSSON. Translated from the Third Edition; with an Introduction by Sir J. LUBBOCK. 8vo. with Plates. [*Nearly ready.*

The **LAKE DWELLINGS** of **SWITZERLAND** and other parts of Europe. By Dr. F. KELLER. Translated and arranged by J. E. LEE, F.S.A. F.G.S. With Woodcuts and nearly 100 Plates of Figures. Royal 8vo. 31s. 6d.

BIBLE ANIMALS; being an Account of the various Birds, Beasts, Fishes, and other Animals mentioned in the Holy Scriptures. By the Rev. J. G. WOOD, M.A. F.L.S. Copiously illustrated with Original Designs, made under the Author's superintendence and engraved on Wood. In course of publication monthly, to be completed in 20 Parts, price 1s. each, forming One Volume, uniform with 'Homes without Hands.'

HOMES WITHOUT HANDS: a Description of the Habitations of Animals, classed according to their Principle of Construction. By Rev. J. G. WOOD, M.A. F.L.S. With about 140 Vignettes on Wood (20 full size of page). Second Edition. 8vo. 21s.

MANUAL of **CORALS** and **SEA JELLIES**. By J. R. GREENE, B.A. Edited by the Rev. J. A. GALBRAITH, M.A. and the Rev. S. HAUGHTON, M.D. Fcp. with 39 Woodcuts, 5s.

Manual of Sponges and Animalculæ; with a General Introduction on the Principles of Zoology. By the same Author and Editors. Fcp. with 16 Woodcuts, 2s.

Manual of the Metalloids. By J. APJOHN, M.D. F.R.S. and the same Editors. Revised Edition. Fcp. with 38 Woodcuts, 7s. 6d.

The **HARMONIES** of **NATURE** and **UNITY** of **CREATION**. By Dr. GEORGE HARTWIG. 8vo. with numerous Illustrations, 18s.

The **Sea and its Living Wonders.** By the same Author. Third (English) Edition. 8vo. with many Illustrations, 21s.

The **Tropical World.** By the same Author. With 8 Chromoxylographs and 172 Woodcuts. 8vo. 21s.

The **POLAR WORLD**; a Popular Account of Nature and Man in the Arctic and Antarctic Regions By the same Author. 8vo. with numerous Illustrations. [*Nearly ready.*

A FAMILIAR HISTORY of BIRDS By E. STANLEY, D.D. F.R.S. late Lord Bishop of Norwich. Seventh Edition, with Woodcuts. Fcp. 3s. 6d.

CEYLON. By Sir J. EMERSON TENNENT, K.C.S. LL.D. Fifth Edition; with Maps, &c. and 90 Wood Engravings. 2 vols. 8vo. £2 10s.

The Wild Elephant, its Structure and Habits, with the Method of Taking and Training it in Ceylon. By the same Author. Fcp. 8vo. with 22 Woodcuts, 3s. 6d.

KIRBY and SPENCE'S INTRODUCTION to ENTOMOLOGY, or Elements of the Natural History of Insects. 7th Edition. Crown 8vo. 5s.

MAUNDER'S TREASURY of NATURAL HISTORY, or Popular Dictionary of Zoology. Revised and corrected by T. S. COBBOLD, M.D Fcp. with 900 Woodcuts, 10s.

The TREASURY of BOTANY, or Popular Dictionary of the Vegetable Kingdom; including a Glossary of Botanical Terms. Edited by J. LINDLEY, F.R.S. and T. MOORE, F.L.S. assisted by eminent Contributors. Pp. 1,274, with 274 Woodcuts and 20 Steel Plates. 2 Parts, fcp. 20s.

The ELEMENTS of BOTANY for FAMILIES and SCHOOLS. Tenth Edition, revised by THOMAS MOORE, F.L.S. Fcp. with 154 Woodcuts, 2s. 6d.

The ROSE AMATEUR'S GUIDE. By THOMAS RIVERS. Twelfth Edition. Fcp. 4s.

The BRITISH FLORA; comprising the Phænogamous or Flowering Plants and the Ferns. By Sir W. J. HOOKER, K.H. and G. A. WALKER-ARNOTT, LL.D. 12mo. with 12 Plates, 14s. or coloured, 21s.

LOUDON'S ENCYCLOPÆDIA of PLANTS; comprising the Specific Character, Description, Culture, History, &c. of all the Plants found in Great Britain. With upwards of 12,000 Woodcuts. 8vo. 42s.

Loudon's Encyclopædia of Trees and Shrubs; containing the Hardy Trees and Shrubs of Great Britain scientifically and popularly described. With 2,000 Woodcuts. 8vo. 50s.

MAUNDER'S SCIENTIFIC and LITERARY TREASURY. New Edition, thoroughly revised and in great part re-written, with above 1,000 new Articles, by J. Y. JOHNSON, Corr. M.Z.S. Fcp. 10s. 6d.

A DICTIONARY of SCIENCE, LITERATURE, and ART. Fourth Edition, re-edited by W. T. BRANDE (the Author), and GEORGE W. COX, M.A. assisted by contributors of eminent Scientific and Literary Acquirements. 3 vols. medium 8vo. price 63s. cloth.

ESSAYS from the EDINBURGH and QUARTERLY REVIEWS. By Sir J. F. W. HERSCHEL, Bart. M.A. 8vo. 18s.

Chemistry, Medicine, Surgery, and the *Allied Sciences.*

A DICTIONARY of CHEMISTRY and the Allied Branches of other Sciences; founded on that of the late Dr. Ure. By HENRY WATTS, F.C.S. assisted by eminent Contributors. 5 vols. medium 8vo. in course of publication in Parts. VOL. I. 31s. 6d. VOL. II. 26s. VOL. III. 31s. 6d. VOL. IV. 24s. are now ready

ELEMENTS of CHEMISTRY, Theoretical and Practical. By WILLIAM A. MILLER, M.D. LL.D. F.R.S. F.G.S. Prof. of Chemistry, King's Coll. London. 3 vols. 8vo. £3. PART I. CHEMICAL PHYSICS, 15s. PART II. INORGANIC CHEMISTRY, 21s. PART III. ORGANIC CHEMISTRY, 24s.

A MANUAL of CHEMISTRY, Descriptive and Theoretical. By WILLIAM ODLING, M.B. F.R.S. PART I. 8vo. 9s. PART II. *just ready.*

A Course of Practical Chemistry, for the use of Medical Students. By the same Author. New Edition, with 70 Woodcuts. Crown 8vo. 7s. 6d.

Lectures on Animal Chemistry, delivered at the Royal College of Physicians in 1865. By the same Author. Crown 8vo. 4s. 6d.

HANDBOOK of CHEMICAL ANALYSIS, adapted to the UNITARY *System* of Notation. By F. T. CONINGTON, M.A. F.C.S. Post 8vo. 7s. 6d. —CONINGTON'S *Tables of Qualitative Analysis*, price 2s. 6d.

The DIAGNOSIS, PATHOLOGY, and TREATMENT of DISEASES of Women; including the Diagnosis of Pregnancy. By GRAILY HEWITT, M.D. Second Edition, enlarged; with 116 Woodcut Illustrations. 8vo. 24s.

LECTURES on the DISEASES of INFANCY and CHILDHOOD. By CHARLES WEST, M.D. &c. Fifth Edition, revised and enlarged. 8vo. 16s.

EXPOSITION of the SIGNS and SYMPTOMS of PREGNANCY: with other Papers on subjects connected with Midwifery. By W. F. MONTGOMERY, M.A. M.D. M.R.I.A. 8vo. with Illustrations, 25s.

A SYSTEM of SURGERY, Theoretical and Practical. In Treatises by Various Authors. Edited by T. HOLMES, M.A. Cantab. Assistant-Surgeon to St. George's Hospital. 4 vols. 8vo. £4 13s.

Vol. I. General Pathology. 21s.

Vol. II. Local Injuries: Gunshot Wounds, Injuries of the Head, Back, Face, Neck, Chest, Abdomen, Pelvis, of the Upper and Lower Extremities, and Diseases of the Eye. 21s.

Vol. III. Operative Surgery. Diseases of the Organs of Circulation, Locomotion, &c. 21s.

Vol. IV. Diseases of the Organs of Digestion, of the Genito-Urinary System, and of the Breast, Thyroid Gland, and Skin; with APPENDIX and GENERAL INDEX. 30s.

LECTURES on the PRINCIPLES and PRACTICE of PHYSIC. By THOMAS WATSON, M.D. New Edition in preparation.

LECTURES on SURGICAL PATHOLOGY. By J. PAGET, F.R.S. Edited by W. TURNER, M.B. New Edition in preparation.

A TREATISE on the CONTINUED FEVERS of GREAT BRITAIN. By C. MURCHISON, M.D. 8vo. with coloured Plates, 18s.

ANATOMY, DESCRIPTIVE and SURGICAL. By HENRY GRAY, F.R.S. With 410 Wood Engravings from Dissections. Fourth Edition, by T. HOLMES, M.A. Cantab. Royal 8vo. 28s.

OUTLINES of PHYSIOLOGY, Human and Comparative. By JOHN MARSHALL, F.R.C.S. Surgeon to the University College Hospital. 2 vols. crown 8vo. with 122 Woodcuts, 32s.

The CYCLOPÆDIA of ANATOMY and PHYSIOLOGY. Edited by the late R. B. TODD, M.D. F.R.S. 5 vols. 8vo. with 2,853 Woodcuts, £6 6s.

PHYSIOLOGICAL ANATOMY and PHYSIOLOGY of MAN. By the late R. B. TODD, M.D. F.R.S. and W. BOWMAN, F.R.S. of King's College. With numerous Illustrations. VOL. II. 8vo. 25s.
  VOL. I. New Edition by Dr. LIONEL S. BEALE, F.R.S. in course of publication; PART I. with 8 Plates, 7s. 6d.

HISTOLOGICAL DEMONSTRATIONS; a Guide to the Microscopical Examination of the Animal Tissues in Health and Disease, for the use of the Medical and Veterinary Professions. By G. HARLEY, M.D. and G. T. BROWN, M.R.C.V.S. Post 8vo. with 223 Woodcuts, price 12s.

COPLAND'S DICTIONARY of PRACTICAL MEDICINE, abridged from the larger work and throughout brought down to the present State of Medical Science. 8vo. 36s.

The WORKS of SIR B. C. BRODIE, Bart. collected and arranged by CHARLES HAWKINS, F.R.C.S.E. 3 vols. 8vo. with Medallion and Facsimile. 48s.

The TOXICOLOGIST'S GUIDE: a New Manual on Poisons, giving the Best Methods to be pursued for the Detection of Poisons (post-mortem or otherwise). By JOHN HORSLEY, F.C.S. Analytical Chemist. Post 8vo. 3s. 6d.

A MANUAL of MATERIA MEDICA and THERAPEUTICS, abridged from Dr. PEREIRA'S *Elements* by F. J. FARRE, M.D. assisted by R. BENTLEY, M.R.C.S. and by R. WARINGTON, F.R.S. 8vo. with 90 Woodcuts, 21s.

THOMSON'S CONSPECTUS of the BRITISH PHARMACOPŒIA, Corrected by E. LLOYD BIRKETT, M.D. 18mo. price 5s. 6d.

MANUAL of the DOMESTIC PRACTICE of MEDICINE. By W. B KESTEVEN, F.R.C.S.E. Third Edition, revised, with Additions. Fcp. 5s.

GYMNASTS and GYMNASTICS. By JOHN H. HOWARD, late Professor of Gymnastics, Comm. Coll. Ripponden. Second Edition, revised and enlarged, with 135 Woodcuts. Crown 8vo. 10s. 6d.

The Fine Arts, and *Illustrated Editions.*

HALF-HOUR LECTURES on the HISTORY and PRACTICE of the Fine and Ornamental Arts. By WILLIAM B. SCOTT. New Edition, revised by the Author; with 50 Woodcuts. Crown 8vo. 8s. 6d.

An INTRODUCTION to the STUDY of NATIONAL MUSIC; comprising Researches into Popular Songs, Traditions, and Customs. By CARL ENGEL. With numerous Musical Specimens. 8vo. 16s.

LECTURES on the HISTORY of MODERN MUSIC, delivered at the Royal Institution. By JOHN HULLAH. FIRST COURSE, with Chronological Tables, post 8vo. 6s. 6d. SECOND COURSE, on the Transition Period, with 40 Specimens, 8vo. 16s.

SIX LECTURES on HARMONY, delivered at the Royal Institution of Great Britain before Easter 1867. By G. A. MACFARREN. With numerous engraved Musical Examples and Specimens. 8vo. 10s. 6d.

The **CHORALE BOOK** for **ENGLAND**: the Hymns translated by Miss C. WINKWORTH; the tunes arranged by Prof. W. S. BENNETT and OTTO GOLDSCHMIDT. Fcp. 4to. 12s. 6d.

Congregational Edition. Fcp. 2s.

SACRED MUSIC for **FAMILY USE**; a Selection of Pieces for One, Two, or more Voices, from the best Composers, Foreign and English. Edited by JOHN HULLAH. 1 vol. music folio, price 21s.

The **NEW TESTAMENT**, illustrated with Wood Engravings after the Early Masters, chiefly of the Italian School. Crown 4to. 63s. cloth, gilt top; or £5 5s. elegantly bound in morocco.

LYRA GERMANICA; the Christian Year. Translated by CATHERINE WINKWORTH; with 125 Illustrations on Wood drawn by J. LEIGHTON, F.S.A. 4to. 21s.

LYRA GERMANICA; the Christian Life. Translated by CATHERINE WINKWORTH; with about 200 Woodcut Illustrations by J. LEIGHTON, F.S.A. and other Artists. 4to. 21s.

The **LIFE** of **MAN SYMBOLISED** by the **MONTHS of the YEAR**. Text selected by R. PIGOT; Illustrations on Wood from Original Designs by J. LEIGHTON, F.S.A. 4to. 42s.

CATS' and **FARLIE'S MORAL EMBLEMS**; with Aphorisms, Adages, and Proverbs of all Nations. 121 Illustrations on Wood by J. LEIGHTON, F.S.A. Text selected by R. PIGOT. Imperial 8vo. 31s. 6d.

SHAKSPEARE'S SENTIMENTS and **SIMILES**, printed in Black and Gold, and Illuminated in the Missal Style by HENRY NOEL HUMPHREYS. Square post 8vo. 21s.

SACRED and **LEGENDARY ART.** By Mrs. JAMESON.

Legends of the Saints and Martyrs. Fifth Edition, with 19 Etchings and 187 Woodcuts. 2 vols. square crown 8vo. 31s. 6d.

Legends of the Monastic Orders. Third Edition, with 11 Etchings and 88 Woodcuts. 1 vol. square crown 8vo. 21s.

Legends of the Madonna. Third Edition, with 27 Etchings and 165 Woodcuts. 1 vol. square crown 8vo. 21s.

The History of Our Lord, with that of his Types and Precursors. Completed by Lady EASTLAKE. Revised Edition, with 31 Etchings and 281 Woodcuts. 2 vols. square crown 8vo. 42s.

Arts, Manufactures, &c.

DRAWING from **NATURE**. By GEORGE BARNARD, Professor of Drawing at Rugby School. With 18 Lithographic Plates, and 108 Wood Engravings. Imperial 8vo. price 25s. Or in Three Parts, royal 8vo. Part I. *Trees and Foliage*, 7s. 6d. Part II. *Foreground Studies*, 7s. 6d. Part III. *Tour in Switzerland and the Pyrenees*, 7s. 6d.

GWILT'S ENCYCLOPÆDIA of ARCHITECTURE, with above 1,100 Engravings on Wood. Fifth Edition, revised and enlarged by WYATT PAPWORTH. Additionally illustrated with nearly 400 Wood Engravings by O. Jewitt, and more than 100 other new Woodcuts. 8vo. 52s. 6d.

TUSCAN SCULPTORS, their Lives, Works, and Times. With 45 Etchings and 28 Woodcuts from Original Drawings and Photographs. By CHARLES C. PERKINS. 2 vols. imperial 8vo. 63s.

ORIGINAL DESIGNS for WOOD-CARVING, with PRACTICAL IN- structions in the Art. By A. F. B. With 20 Plates of Illustrations engraved on Wood. 4to. 18s.

HINTS on HOUSEHOLD TASTE in FURNITURE and DECORATION. By CHARLES L. EASTLAKE, Architect. With numerous Illustrations engraved on Wood. [*Nearly ready.*

The ENGINEER'S HANDBOOK; explaining the Principles which should guide the Young Engineer in the Construction of Machinery. By C. S. LOWNDES. Post 8vo. 5s.

The ELEMENTS of MECHANISM. By T. M. GOODEVE, M.A. Professor of Mechanics at the R. M. Acad. Woolwich. Second Edition, with 217 Woodcuts. Post 8vo. 6s. 6d.

URE'S DICTIONARY of ARTS, MANUFACTURES, and MINES. Sixth Edition, chiefly rewritten and greatly enlarged by ROBERT HUNT, F.R.S. assisted by numerous Contributors eminent in Science and the Arts, and familiar with Manufactures. With above 2,000 Woodcuts. 3 vols. medium 8vo. price £4 14s. 6d.

ENCYCLOPÆDIA of CIVIL ENGINEERING, Historical, Theoretical, and Practical. By E. CRESY, C.E. With above 3,000 Woodcuts. 8vo. 42s.

TREATISE on MILLS and MILLWORK. By W. FAIRBAIRN, C.E. Second Edition, with 18 Plates and 322 Woodcuts. 2 vols. 8vo. 32s.

Useful Information for Engineers. By the same Author. FIRST, SECOND, and THIRD SERIES, with many Plates and Woodcuts. 3 vols. crown 8vo. 10s. 6d. each.

The Application of Cast and Wrought Iron to Building Purposes. By the same Author. Third Edition, with 6 Plates and 118 Woodcuts. 8vo. 16s.

IRON SHIP BUILDING, its History and Progress, as comprised in a Series of Experimental Researches. By the same Author. With 4 Plates and 130 Woodcuts. 8vo. 18s.

A TREATISE on the STEAM ENGINE, in its various Applications to Mines, Mills, Steam Navigation, Railways and Agriculture. By J. BOURNE, C.E. New Edition; with 37 Plates and 546 Woodcuts. 4to. 42s.

Catechism of the Steam Engine, in its various Applications to Mines, Mills, Steam Navigation, Railways, and Agriculture. By the same Author. With 199 Woodcuts. Fcp. 6s.

Handbook of the Steam Engine. By the same Author, forming a KEY to the Catechism of the Steam Engine, with 67 Woodcuts. Fcp. 9s.

A TREATISE on the SCREW PROPELLER, SCREW VESSELS, and Screw Engines, as adapted for purposes of Peace and War; with Notices of other Methods of Propulsion, Tables of the Dimensions and Performance of Screw Steamers, and detailed Specifications of Ships and Engines. By J. BOURNE, C.E. 3rd Edition, with 54 Plates and 287 Woodcuts. 4to. 63s.

A HISTORY of the MACHINE-WROUGHT HOSIERY and LACE Manufactures. By WILLIAM FELKIN, F.L.S. F.S.S. Royal 8vo. 21s

MANUAL of PRACTICAL ASSAYING, for the use of Metallurgists, Captains of Mines, and Assayers in general. By JOHN MITCHELL, F.C.S. Second Edition, with 360 Woodcuts. 8vo. 21s.

The ART of PERFUMERY; the History and Theory of Odours, and the Methods of Extracting the Aromas of Plants. By Dr. PIESSE, F.C.S. Third Edition, with 53 Woodcuts. Crown 8vo. 10s. 6d.

Chemical, Natural, and Physical Magic, for Juveniles during the Holidays. By the same Author. Third Edition, with 38 Woodcuts. Fcp. 6s.

LOUDON'S ENCYCLOPÆDIA of AGRICULTURE: comprising the Laying-out, Improvement, and Management of Landed Property, and the Cultivation and Economy of the Productions of Agriculture. With 1,100 Woodcuts. 8vo. 31s. 6d.

Loudon's Encylopædia of Gardening: comprising the Theory and Practice of Horticulture, Floriculture, Arboriculture, and Landscape Gardening. With 1,000 Woodcuts. 8vo. 31s. 6d.

Loudon's Encyclopædia of Cottage, Farm, and Villa Architecture and Furniture. With more than 2,000 Woodcuts. 8vo. 42s.

BAYLDON'S ART of VALUING RENTS and TILLAGES, and Claims of Tenants upon Quitting Farms, both at Michaelmas and Lady-Day. Eighth Edition, revised by J. C. MORTON. 8vo. 10s. 6d.

Religious and *Moral Works*.

An EXPOSITION of the 39 ARTICLES, Historical and Doctrinal. By E. HAROLD BROWNE, D.D. Lord Bishop of Ely. Seventh Edit. 8vo. 16s.

The ACTS of the APOSTLES; with a Commentary, and Practical and Devotional Suggestions for Readers and Students of the English Bible. By the Rev. F. C. COOK, M.A. Canon of Exeter, &c. New Edition. 8vo. 12s. 6d.

The LIFE and EPISTLES of ST. PAUL. By W. J. CONYBEARE, M.A. late Fellow of Trin. Coll.Cantab. and the Very Rev. J. S. HOWSON, D.D. Dean of Chester.

LIBRARY EDITION, with all the Original Illustrations, Maps, Landscapes on Steel, Woodcuts, &c. 2 vols. 4to. 48s.

INTERMEDIATE EDITION, with a Selection of Maps, Plates, and Woodcuts. 2 vols. square crown 8vo. 31s. 6d.

PEOPLE'S EDITION, revised and condensed, with 46 Illustrations and Maps. 2 vols. crown 8vo. 12s.

The VOYAGE and SHIPWRECK of ST. PAUL; with Dissertations on the Life and Writings of St. Luke and the Ships and Navigation of the Ancients. By JAMES SMITH, F.R.S. Third Edition. Crown 8vo. 10s. 6d.

EVIDENCE of the TRUTH of the CHRISTIAN RELIGION derived from the Literal Fulfilment of Prophecy. By ALEXANDER KEITH, D.D. 37th Edition, with numerous Plates, in square 8vo. 12s. 6d.; also the 39th Edition, in post 8vo. with 5 Plates, 6s.

The HISTORY and DESTINY of the WORLD and of the CHURCH, according to Scripture. By the same Author. Square 8vo. with 40 Illustrations, 10s.

A CRITICAL and GRAMMATICAL COMMENTARY on ST. PAUL'S
Epistles. By C. J. ELLICOTT, D.D. Lord Bishop of Gloucester and Bristol. 8vo.
Galatians, Third Edition, 8s. 6d.
Ephesians, Fourth Edition, 8s. 6d.
Pastoral Epistles, Third Edition, 10s. 6d.
Philippians, Colossians, and Philemon, Third Edition, 10s. 6d.
Thessalonians, Third Edition, 7s. 6d.

Historical Lectures on the Life of our Lord Jesus Christ: being the Hulsean Lectures for 1859. By the same Author. Fourth Edition. 8vo. price 10s. 6d.

An INTRODUCTION to the STUDY of the NEW TESTAMENT, Critical, Exegetical, and Theological. By the Rev. S. DAVIDSON, D.D. LL.D 2 vols. 8vo. [*In the press.*

Rev. T. H. HORNE'S INTRODUCTION to the CRITICAL STUDY and Knowledge of the Holy Scriptures. Eleventh Edition, corrected and extended under careful Editorial revision. With 4 Maps and 22 Woodcuts and Facsimiles. 4 vols. 8vo. £3 13s. 6d.

Rev. T. H. Horne's Compendious Introduction to the Study of the Bible, being an Analysis of the larger work by the same Author. Re-edited by the Rev. JOHN AYRE, M.A. With Maps, &c. Post 8vo. 9s.

EWALD'S HISTORY of ISRAEL to the DEATH of MOSES. Translated from the German. Edited, with a Preface, by RUSSELL MARTINEAU, M.A. Prof. of Hebrew in Manchester New Coll. London. 8vo. 18s.

The TREASURY of BIBLE KNOWLEDGE; being a Dictionary of the Books, Persons, Places, Events, and other matters of which mention is made in Holy Scripture. By Rev. J. AYRE, M.A. With Maps, 16 Plates, and numerous Woodcuts. Fcp. 10s. 6d.

The LIFE and REIGN of DAVID KING of ISRAEL. By GEORGE SMITH, LLD. F.A.S. Crown 8vo. 7s. 6d.

The GREEK TESTAMENT; with Notes, Grammatical and Exegetical. By the Rev. W. WEBSTER, M.A. and the Rev. W. F. WILKINSON, M.A. 2 vols. 8vo. £2 4s.
   VOL. I. the Gospels and Acts, 20s.
   VOL. II. the Epistles and Apocalypse, 24s.

EVERY-DAY SCRIPTURE DIFFICULTIES explained and illustrated. By J. E. PRESCOTT, M.A. VOL. I. *Matthew* and *Mark*; VOL. II. *Luke* and *John*. 2 vols. 8vo. 9s. each.

The PENTATEUCH and BOOK of JOSHUA CRITICALLY EXAMINED. By the Right Rev. J. W. COLENSO, D.D. Lord Bishop of Natal. People's Edition, in 1 vol. crown 8vo. 6s. or in 5 Parts, 1s. each.

The CHURCH and the WORLD: Essays on Questions of the Day. By Various Writers. Edited by the Rev. ORBY SHIPLEY, M.A. FIRST SERIES, Third Edition, 8vo. 15s. SECOND SERIES, 8vo. 15s. THIRD SERIES preparing for publication.

TRACTS for the DAY; a Series of Essays on Theological Subjects. By various Authors. Edited by the Rev. ORBY SHIPLEY, M.A. I. *Priestly Absolution Scriptural*, 9d. II. *Purgatory*, 9d. III. *The Seven Sacraments*, 1s. 6d. IV. *Miracles and Prayer*, 6d. V. *The Real Presence*, 1s. 3d. VI. *Casuistry*, 1s. VII. *Unction of the Sick*, 9d. VIII. *The Rule of Worship*, 9d. IX. *Popular Rationalism*, 9d.

The FORMATION of CHRISTENDOM. PART I. By T. W. ALLIES, 8vo. 12s.

CHRISTENDOM'S DIVISIONS, PART I., a Philosophical Sketch of the Divisions of the Christian Family in East and West. By EDMUND S. FFOULKES. Post 8vo. price 7s. 6d.

Christendom's Divisions, PART II. Greeks and Latins, being a History of their Dissensions and Overtures for Peace down to the Reformation. By the same Author. Post 8vo. 15s.

The HIDDEN WISDOM of CHRIST and the KEY of KNOWLEDGE; or, History of the Apocrypha. By ERNEST DE BUNSEN. 2 vols. 8vo. 28s.

The KEYS of ST. PETER; or, the House of Rechab, connected with the History of Symbolism and Idolatry. By the same Author. 8vo. 14s.

ESSAYS on RELIGION and LITERATURE. Edited by Archbishop MANNING, D.D. 8vo. 10s. 6d. SECOND SERIES, price 14s.

The TEMPORAL MISSION of the HOLY GHOST; or, Reason and Revelation. By Archbishop MANNING, D.D. Second Edit. Cr. 8vo. 8s. 6d.

ENGLAND and CHRISTENDOM. By the same Author. Post 8vo. price 10s. 6d.

ESSAYS and REVIEWS. By the Rev. W. TEMPLE, D.D. the Rev. R. WILLIAMS, B.D. the Rev. B. POWELL, M.A. the Rev. H. B. WILSON, B.D. C. W. GOODWIN, M.A. the Rev. M. PATTISON, B.D. and the Rev. B. JOWETT, M.A. Twelfth Edition. Fcp. 8vo. 5s.

The CATHOLIC DOCTRINE of the ATONEMENT: an Historical Inquiry into its Development in the Church. By H. N. OXENHAM, M.A. 8vo. 8s. 6d.

PASSING THOUGHTS on RELIGION. By ELIZABETH M. SEWELL, Author of 'Amy Herbert.' New Edition. Fcp. 8vo. 5s.

Self-Examination before Confirmation. By the same Author. 32mo. price 1s. 6d.

Readings for a Month Preparatory to Confirmation, from Writers of the Early and English Church. By the same Author. Fcp. 4s.

Readings for Every Day in Lent, compiled from the Writings of Bishop JEREMY TAYLOR. By the same Author. Fcp. 5s.

Preparation for the Holy Communion; the Devotions chiefly from the works of JEREMY TAYLOR. By the same. 32mo. 3s.

PRINCIPLES of EDUCATION Drawn from Nature and Revelation, and applied to Female Education in the Upper Classes. By the Author of 'Amy Herbert.' 2 vols. fcp. 12s. 6d.

NEW WORKS PUBLISHED BY LONGMANS AND CO. 21

The **WIFE'S MANUAL**; or, Prayers, Thoughts, and Songs on Several Occasions of a Matron's Life. By the Rev. W. CALVERT, M.A. Crown 8vo. price 10s. 6d.

'**SPIRITUAL SONGS**' for the **SUNDAYS** and **HOLIDAYS** throughout the Year. By J. S. B. MONSELL, LL.D. Vicar of Egham and Rural Dean. Sixth Thousand. Fcp. 4s. 6d.

The **Beatitudes**: Abasement before God; Sorrow for Sin; Meekness of Spirit; Desire for Holiness; Gentleness; Purity of Heart; the Peacemakers; Sufferings for Christ. By the same. Third Edition. Fcp. 3s. 6d.

His **PRESENCE—not his MEMORY, 1855.** By the same Author, in Memory of his SON. Fifth Edition. 16mo. 1s.

LYRA DOMESTICA; Christian Songs for Domestic Edification. Translated from the *Psaltery and Harp* of C. J. P. SPITTA, and from other sources, by RICHARD MASSIE. FIRST and SECOND SERIES, fcp. 4s. 6d. each.

LYRA SACRA; Hymns, Ancient and Modern, Odes and Fragments of Sacred Poetry. Edited by the Rev. B. W. SAVILE, M.A. Third Edition, enlarged and improved. Fcp. 5s.

LYRA GERMANICA, translated from the German by Miss C. WINKWORTH. FIRST SERIES, Hymns for the Sundays and Chief Festivals; SECOND SERIES, the Christian Life. Fcp. 3s. 6d. each SERIES.

LYRA EUCHARISTICA; Hymns and Verses on the Holy Communion, Ancient and Modern: with other Poems. Edited by the Rev. ORBY SHIPLEY, M.A. Second Edition. Fcp. 7s. 6d.

Lyra **Messianica**; Hymns and Verses on the Life of Christ, Ancient and Modern; with other Poems. By the same Editor. Second Edition, altered and enlarged. Fcp. 7s. 6d.

Lyra **Mystica**; Hymns and Verses on Sacred Subjects, Ancient and Modern. By the same Editor. Fcp. 7s. 6d.

ENDEAVOURS after the **CHRISTIAN LIFE**: Discourses. By JAMES MARTINEAU. Fourth and cheaper Edition, carefully revised; the Two Series complete in One Volume. Post 8vo. 7s. 6d.

WHATELY'S Introductory Lessons on the Christian Evidences. 18mo. 6d.

INTRODUCTORY LESSONS on the **HISTORY of RELIGIOUS** Worship; being a Sequel to the 'Lessons on Christian Evidences.' By RICHARD WHATELY, D.D. New Edition. 18mo. 2s. 6d.

MOSHEIM'S ECCLESIASTICAL HISTORY. MURDOCK and SOAMES'S Translation and Notes, re-edited by the Rev. W. STUBBS, M.A. 3 vols. 8vo. 45s.

BISHOP JEREMY TAYLOR'S ENTIRE WORKS: With Life by BISHOP HEBER. Revised and corrected by the Rev. C. P. EDEN, 10 vols. price £5 5s.

Travels, Voyages, &c.

The **NORTH-WEST PENINSULA of ICELAND**; being the Journal of a Tour in Iceland in the Summer of 1862. By C. W. SHEPHERD, M.A. F.Z.S. With a Map and Two Illustrations. Fcp. 8vo. 7s. 6d.

PICTURES in **TYROL** and **Elsewhere**. From a Family Sketch-Book. By the Authoress of 'A Voyage en Zigzag,' &c. 4to. with numerous Illustrations, 21s.

HOW WE SPENT the SUMMER; or, a Voyage en Zigzag in Switzerland and Tyrol with some Members of the ALPINE CLUB. From the Sketch-Book of one of the Party. In oblong 4to. with 300 Illustrations, 15s.

BEATEN TRACKS; or, Pen and Pencil Sketches in Italy. By the Authoress of 'A Voyage en Zigzag.' With 42 Plates, containing about 200 Sketches from Drawings made on the Spot. 8vo. 16s.

MAP of the **CHAIN of MONT BLANC**, from an actual Survey in 1863—1864. By A. ADAMS-REILLY, F.R.G.S. M.A.C. Published under the Authority of the Alpine Club. In Chromolithography on extra stout drawing-paper 28in. × 17in. price 10s. or mounted on canvas in a folding case, 12s. 6d.

HISTORY of **DISCOVERY** in our **AUSTRALASIAN COLONIES**, Australia, Tasmania, and New Zealand, from the Earliest Date to the Present Day. By WILLIAM HOWITT. 2 vols. 8vo. with 3 Maps, 20s.

The **CAPITAL** of the **TYCOON**; a Narrative of a Three Years' Residence in Japan. By Sir RUTHERFORD ALCOCK, K.C.B. 2 vols. 8vo. with numerous Illustrations, 42s.

FLORENCE, the **NEW CAPITAL of ITALY**. By C. R. WELD. With several Woodcuts from Drawings by the Author. Post 8vo. 12s. 6d.

The **DOLOMITE MOUNTAINS**; Excursions through Tyrol, Carinthia, Carniola, and Friuli, 1861-1863. By J. GILBERT and G. C. CHURCHILL, F.R.G.S. With numerous Illustrations. Square crown 8vo. 21s.

A LADY'S TOUR ROUND MONTE ROSA; including Visits to the Italian Valleys. With Map and Illustrations. Post 8vo. 14s.

GUIDE to the **PYRENEES**, for the use of Mountaineers. By CHARLES PACKE. 2d Edition, with Map and Illustrations. Cr. 8vo. 7s. 6d.

The **ALPINE GUIDE**. By JOHN BALL, M.R.I.A. late President of the Alpine Club. Post 8vo. with Maps and other Illustrations.

Guide to the Eastern Alps, *nearly ready*.

Guide to the Western Alps, including Mont Blanc, Monte Rosa, Zermatt, &c. 7s. 6d.

Guide to the Oberland and all Switzerland, excepting the Neighbourhood of Monte Rosa and the Great St. Bernard; with Lombardy and the adjoining portion of Tyrol. 7s. 6d.

NARRATIVES of SHIPWRECKS of the ROYAL NAVY between 1793 and 1857, compiled from Official Documents in the Admiralty by W. O. S. GILLY; with a Preface by W. S. GILLY, D.D. Third Edition. Fcp. 5s.

The **ARCH of TITUS** and the **SPOILS** of the **TEMPLE**; an Historical and Critical Lecture, with Authentic Illustrations. By WILLIAM KNIGHT, M.A. With 10 Woodcuts from Ancient Remains. 4to. 10s.

A **WEEK** at the **LAND'S END**. By J. T. BLIGHT; assisted by E. H. RODD, R. Q. COUCH, and J. RALFS. With Map and 96 Woodcuts. Fcp. price 6s. 6d.

CURIOSITIES of **LONDON**; exhibiting the most Rare and Remarkable Objects of Interest in the Metropolis; with nearly Sixty Years' Personal Recollections. By JOHN TIMBS, F.S.A. New Edition, corrected and enlarged. 8vo. with Portrait, 21s.

VISITS to **REMARKABLE PLACES**: Old Halls, Battle-Fields, and Scenes Illustrative of Striking Passages in English History and Poetry. By WILLIAM HOWITT. 2 vols. square crown 8vo. with Woodcuts, 25s.

The **RURAL LIFE** of **ENGLAND**. By the same Author. With Woodcuts by Bewick and Williams. Medium 8vo. 12s. 6d.

The **ENGLISHMAN** in **INDIA**. By CHARLES RAIKES, Esq. C.S.I. formerly Commissioner of Lahore. Post 8vo. 7s. 6d.

The **IRISH** in **AMERICA**. By JOHN FRANCIS MAGUIRE, M.P. for Cork. Post 8vo. 12s. 6d.

Works of *Fiction*.

The **WARDEN**: a Novel. By ANTHONY TROLLOPE. Crown 8vo. 2s. 6d.

Barchester Towers: a Sequel to 'The Warden.' By the same Author. Crown 8vo. 3s. 6d.

SPRINGDALE ABBEY: Extracts from the Letters of an ENGLISH PREACHER. 8vo. 12s.

TALES and **STORIES** by ELIZABETH M. SEWELL, Author of 'Amy Herbert,' uniform Edition, each Story or Tale complete in a single Volume.

AMY HERBERT, 2s. 6d.	IVORS, 3s. 6d.
GERTRUDE, 2s. 6d.	KATHARINE ASHTON, 3s. 6d.
EARL'S DAUGHTER, 2s. 6d.	MARGARET PERCIVAL, 5s.
EXPERIENCE OF LIFE, 2s. 6d.	LANETON PARSONAGE, 4s. 6d.
CLEVE HALL, 3s. 6d.	URSULA, 4s. 6d.

A Glimpse of the World. By the Author of 'Amy Herbert.' Fcp. 7s. 6d.

The Journal of a Home Life. By the same Author. Post 8vo. 9s. 6d.

After Life; a Sequel to 'The Journal of a Home Life.' By the same Author. Post 8vo. [*Nearly ready.*]

BECKER'S GALLUS; or, Roman Scenes of the Time of Augustus: with Notes and Excursuses. New Edition. Post 8vo. 7s. 6d.

BECKER'S CHARICLES; a Tale illustrative of Private Life among the Ancient Greeks: with Notes and Excursuses. New Edition. Post 8vo. 7s. 6d.

NOVELS and TALES by G. J. WHYTE MELVILLE:—

The Gladiators: A Tale of Rome and Judæa. Crown 8vo. 5s.

Digby Grand, an Autobiography. Crown 8vo. 5s.

Kate Coventry, an Autobiography. Crown 8vo. 5s.

General Bounce, or the Lady and the Locusts. Crown 8vo. 5s.

Holmby House, a Tale of Old Northamptonshire. Crown 8vo. 5s.

Good for Nothing, or All Down Hill. Crown 8vo. 6s.

The Queen's Maries, a Romance of Holyrood. Crown 8vo. 6s.

The Interpreter, a Tale of the War. Crown 8vo. 5s.

THE SIX SISTERS of the VALLEYS: an Historical Romance. By W. BRAMLEY-MOORE, M.A. Fourth Edition, with 14 Illustrations. Crown 8vo. 5s.

TALES from GREEK MYTHOLOGY. By GEORGE W. COX, M.A. late Scholar of Trin. Coll. Oxon. Second Edition. Square 16mo. 3s. 6d.

Tales of the Gods and Heroes. By the same Author. Second Edition. Fcp. 5s.

Tales of Thebes and Argos. By the same Author. Fcp. 4s. 6d.

A MANUAL of MYTHOLOGY, in the form of Question and Answer. By the same Author. Fcp. 3s.

Poetry and *The Drama*.

MOORE'S POETICAL WORKS, Cheapest Editions complete in 1 vol. including the Autobiographical Prefaces and Author's last Notes. Crown 8vo. ruby type, with Portrait, 6s.: People's Edition, larger type, 12s. 6d.

Moore's Poetical Works, as above, Library Edition, medium 8vo. with Portrait and Vignette, 14s. or in 10 vols. fcp. 3s. 6d. each.

MOORE'S IRISH MELODIES, Maclise's Edition, with 161 Steel Plates from Original Drawings. Super-royal 8vo. 31s. 6d.

Miniature Edition of Moore's Irish Melodies with Maclise's Designs (as above) reduced in Lithography. Imp. 16mo. 10s. 6d.

MOORE'S LALLA ROOKH. Tenniel's Edition, with 68 Wood Engravings from original Drawings and other Illustrations. Fcp. 4to. 21s.

SOUTHEY'S POETICAL WORKS, with the Author's last Corrections and copyright Additions. Library Edition, in 1 vol. medium 8vo. with Portrait and Vignette, 14s. or in 10 vols. fcp. 3s. 6d. each.

LAYS of ANCIENT ROME; with *Ivry* and the *Armada*. By the Right Hon. LORD MACAULAY. 16mo. 4s. 6d.

Lord Macaulay's Lays of Ancient Rome. With 90 Illustrations on Wood, from the Antique, from Drawings by G. SCHARF. Fcp. 4to. 21s.

Miniature Edition of Lord Macaulay's Lays of Ancient Rome, with the Illustrations (as above) reduced in Lithography. Imp. 16mo. 10s. 6d.

MEMORIES of some CONTEMPORARY POETS; with Selections from their Writings. By EMILY TAYLOR. Royal 18mo. 5s.

POEMS. By JEAN INGELOW. Thirteenth Edition. Fcp. 8vo. 5s.

POEMS by Jean Ingelow. A New Edition, with nearly 100 Illustrations by Eminent Artists, engraved on Wood by the Brothers DALZIEL. Fcp. 4to. 21s.

A STORY of DOOM, and other Poems. By JEAN INGELOW. Fcp. 5s.

POETICAL WORKS of LETITIA ELIZABETH LANDON (L.E.L.) 2 vols. 16mo, 10s.

BOWDLER'S FAMILY SHAKSPEARE, cheaper Genuine Edition, complete in 1 vol. large type, with 36 Woodcut Illustrations, price 14s. or with the same ILLUSTRATIONS, in 6 pocket vols. 3s. 6d. each.

SHAKSPEARE'S SONNETS NEVER BEFORE INTERPRETED; his Private Friends identified; together with a recovered Likeness of Himself. By GERALD MASSEY. 8vo. 18s.

HORATII OPERA. Library Edition, with Marginal References and English Notes. Edited by the Rev. J. E. YONGE. 8vo. 21s.

The ÆNEID of VIRGIL Translated into English Verse. By JOHN CONINGTON, M.A. Crown 8vo. 9s.

ARUNDINES CAMI, sive Musarum Cantabrigiensium Lusus canori. Collegit atque edidit H. DRURY, M.A. Editio Sexta, curavit H. J. HODGSON, M.A. Crown 8vo. 7s. 6d.

EIGHT COMEDIES of ARISTOPHANES, viz. the Acharnians, Knights, Clouds, Wasps, Peace, Birds, Frogs, and Plutus. Translated into Rhymed Metres by LEONARD HAMPSON RUDD, M.A. 8vo. 15s.

PLAYTIME with the POETS: a Selection of the best English Poetry for the use of Children. By a LADY. Revised Edition. Crown 8vo. 5s.

The HOLY CHILD: a Poem in Four Cantos; also an Ode to Silence, and other Poems. By STEPHEN JENNER, M.A. Fcp. 8vo. 5s.

POETICAL WORKS of JOHN EDMUND READE; with final Revision and Additions. 3 vols. fcp. 18s. or each vol. separately, 6s.

The ILIAD of HOMER TRANSLATED into BLANK VERSE. By ICHABOD CHARLES WRIGHT, M.A. 2 vols. crown 8vo. 21s.

The ILIAD of HOMER in ENGLISH HEXAMETER VERSE. By J. HENRY DART, M.A. of Exeter Coll. Oxford. Square crown 8vo. 21s.

DANTE'S DIVINE COMEDY, translated in English Terza Rima by JOHN DAYMAN, M.A. [With the Italian Text, after *Brunetti*, interpaged.] 8vo. 21s.

Rural Sports, &c.

BLAINE'S ENCYCLOPÆDIA of RURAL SPORTS; Hunting, Shooting, Fishing, Racing, &c. With above 600 Woodcuts (20 from Designs by JOHN LEECH). 8vo. 42s.

Col. **HAWKER'S INSTRUCTIONS to YOUNG SPORTSMEN** in all that relates to Guns and Shooting. Revised by the Author's SON. Square crown 8vo. with Illustrations, 18s.

The **RIFLE, its THEORY and PRACTICE.** By ARTHUR WALKER (79th Highlanders), Staff. Hythe and Fleetwood Schools of Musketry. Second Edition. Crown 8vo. with 125 Woodcuts, 5s.

The **DEAD SHOT**, or Sportsman's Complete Guide; a Treatise on the Use of the Gun, Dog-breaking, Pigeon-shooting, &c. By MARKSMAN. Revised Edition. Fcp. 8vo. with Plates, 5s.

The **FLY-FISHER'S ENTOMOLOGY.** By ALFRED RONALDS. With coloured Representations of the Natural and Artificial Insect. Sixth Edition; with 20 coloured Plates. 8vo. 14s.

A **BOOK on ANGLING**; a complete Treatise on the Art of Angling in every branch. By FRANCIS FRANCIS. Second Edition, with Portrait and 15 other Plates, plain and coloured. Post 8vo. 15s.

HANDBOOK of ANGLING: Teaching Fly-fishing, Trolling, Bottom-fishing, Salmon-fishing; with the Natural History of River Fish, and the best modes of Catching them. By EPHEMERA. Fcp. Woodcuts, 5s.

The **BILLIARD BOOK.** By Captain CRAWLEY. With about 100 Diagrams on Steel and Wood. 8vo. 21s.

The **CRICKET FIELD**; or, the History and the Science of the Game of Cricket. By JAMES PYCROFT, B.A. Fourth Edition. Fcp. 5s.

The **HORSE-TRAINER'S and SPORTSMAN'S GUIDE**: with Considerations on the Duties of Grooms, on Purchasing Blood Stock, and on Veterinary Examination. By DIGBY COLLINS. Post 8vo. 6s.

The **HORSE'S FOOT, and HOW to KEEP IT SOUND.** By W. MILES, Esq. Ninth Edition, with Illustrations. Imperial 8vo. 12s. 6d.

A **Plain Treatise on Horse-Shoeing.** By the same Author. Post 8vo. with Illustrations, 2s. 6d.

Stables and Stable-Fittings. By the same. Imp. 8vo. with 13 Plates, 15s.

Remarks on Horses' Teeth, addressed to Purchasers. By the same. Post 8vo. 1s. 6d.

On **DRILL and MANŒUVRES of CAVALRY**, combined with Horse Artillery. By Major-Gen. MICHAEL W. SMITH, C.B. 8vo. 12s. 6d.

BLAINE'S VETERINARY ART; a Treatise on the Anatomy, Physiology, and Curative Treatment of the Diseases of the Horse, Neat Cattle and Sheep. Seventh Edition, revised and enlarged by C. STEEL, M.R.C.V.S.L. 8vo. with Plates and Woodcuts, 18s.

The **HORSE**: with a Treatise on Draught. By WILLIAM YOUATT. New Edition, revised and enlarged. 8vo. with numerous Woodcuts, 12s. 6d.

The **Dog.** By the same Author. 8vo. with numerous Woodcuts, 6s.

The **DOG in HEALTH and DISEASE.** By STONEHENGE. With 70 Wood Engravings. Square crown 8vo. 10s. 6d.

The **GREYHOUND**. By STONEHENGE. Revised Edition, with 24 Portraits of Greyhounds. Square crown 8vo. 21s.

The **OX**; his Diseases and their Treatment: with an Essay on Parturition in the Cow. By J. R. DOBSON. Crown 8vo. with Illustrations. 7s. 6d.

Commerce, Navigation, and *Mercantile Affairs.*

BANKING, CURRENCY, and the EXCHANGES; a Practical Treatise. By ARTHUR CRUMP. Post 8vo. 6s.

The **ELEMENTS of BANKING**. By HENRY DUNNING MACLEOD, M.A. Barrister-at-Law. Post 8vo. [*Nearly ready.*]

The **THEORY and PRACTICE of BANKING**. By the same Author. Second Edition, entirely remodelled. 2 vols. 8vo. 30s.

ELEMENTS of MARITIME INTERNATIONAL LAW. By WILLIAM DE BURGH, B.A. of the Inner Temple, Barrister-at-Law. 8vo. 10s. 6d.

PAPERS on MARITIME LEGISLATION; with a Translation of the German Mercantile Law relating to Maritime Commerce. By ERNST EMIL WENDT. 8vo. 10s. 6d.

PRACTICAL GUIDE for BRITISH SHIPMASTERS to UNITED States Ports. By PIERREPONT EDWARDS. Post 8vo. 8s. 6d.

A **NAUTICAL DICTIONARY**, defining the Technical Language relative to the Building and Equipment of Sailing Vessels and Steamers, &c. By ARTHUR YOUNG. Second Edition; with Plates and 150 Woodcuts. 8vo. 18s.

A **DICTIONARY**, Practical, Theoretical, and Historical, of Commerce and Commercial Navigation. By J. R. M'CULLOCH, Esq. New and thoroughly revised Edition, in the press.

A **MANUAL for NAVAL CADETS**. By J. M'NEIL BOYD, late Captain R.N. Third Edition; with 240 Woodcuts and 11 coloured Plates. Post 8vo. 12s. 6d.

The **LAW of NATIONS** Considered as Independent Political Communities. By TRAVERS TWISS, D.C.L. Regius Professor of Civil Law in the University of Oxford. 2 vols. 8vo. 30s. or separately, PART I. *Peace,* 12s. PART II. *War,* 18s.

Works of Utility and *General Information.*

MODERN COOKERY for PRIVATE FAMILIES, reduced to a System of Easy Practice in a Series of carefully-tested Receipts. By ELIZA ACTON. Newly revised and enlarged Edition; with 8 Plates of Figures and 150 Woodcuts. Fcp. 6s.

On **FOOD** and its **DIGESTION**; an Introduction to Dietetics. By W. BRINTON, M.D. With 48 Woodcuts. Post 8vo. 12s.

WINE, the VINE, and the CELLAR. By THOMAS G. SHAW. Second Edition, revised and enlarged, with 32 Illustrations. 8vo. 16s.

HOW TO BREW GOOD BEER: a complete Guide to the Art of Brewing Ale, Bitter Ale, Table Ale, Brown Stout, Porter, and Table Beer. By JOHN PITT. Revised Edition. Fcp. 4s. 6d.

A PRACTICAL TREATISE on BREWING; with Formulæ for Public Brewers, and Instructions for Private Families. By W. BLACK. 8vo. 10s. 6d.

SHORT WHIST. By MAJOR A. Sixteenth Edition, revised, with an Essay on the Theory of the Modern Scientific Game by PROF. P. Fcp. 3s. 6d.

WHIST, WHAT TO LEAD. By CAM. Fourth Edition. 32mo. 1s.

A HANDBOOK for READERS at the BRITISH MUSEUM. By THOMAS NICHOLS. Post 8vo. 6s.

The EXECUTOR'S GUIDE. By J. C. HUDSON. Enlarged Edition, revised by the Author, with reference to the latest reported Cases and Acts of Parliament. Fcp. 6s.

The CABINET LAWYER; a Popular Digest of the Laws of England, Civil, Criminal, and Constitutional. Twenty-third Edition, brought down to the close of the Parliamentary Session of 1867. Fcp. 10s. 6d.

The PHILOSOPHY of HEALTH; or, an Exposition of the Physiological and Sanitary Conditions conducive to Human Longevity and Happiness. By SOUTHWOOD SMITH, M.D. Eleventh Edition, revised and enlarged; with 113 Woodcuts. 8vo. 7s. 6d.

HINTS to MOTHERS on the MANAGEMENT of their HEALTH during the Period of Pregnancy and in the Lying-in Room. By T. BULL, M.D. Fcp. 5s.

The Maternal Management of Children in Health and Disease. By the same Author. Fcp. 5s.

The LAW RELATING to BENEFIT BUILDING SOCIETIES; with Practical Observations on the Act and all the Cases decided thereon; also a Form of Rules and Forms of Mortgages. By W. TIDD PRATT, Barrister. Second Edition. Fcp. 3s. 6d.

NOTES on HOSPITALS. By FLORENCE NIGHTINGALE. Third Edition, enlarged; with 13 Plans. Post 4to. 18s.

COULTHART'S DECIMAL INTEREST TABLES at 24 Different Rates not exceeding 5 per Cent. Calculated for the use of Bankers. To which are added Commission Tables at One-Eighth and One-Fourth per Cent. 8vo. 15s.

MAUNDER'S TREASURY of KNOWLEDGE and LIBRARY of Reference: comprising an English Dictionary and Grammar, Universal Gazetteer, Classical Dictionary, Chronology, Law Dictionary, a Synopsis of the Peerage, useful Tables, &c. Revised Edition. Fcp. 10s. 6d.

INDEX.

Acton's Modern Cookery 27
Alcock's Residence in Japan 22
Allies on Formation of Christendom 20
Alpine Guide (The) 22
Alvensleben's Maximilian in Mexico 5
Apjohn's Manual of the Metalloids 12
Arnold's Manual of English Literature.... 7
Arnott's Elements of Physics.............. 11
Arundines Cami 25
Autumn holidays of a Country Parson .. 8
Ayre's Treasury of Bible Knowledge...... 19

Bacon's Essays, by Whately 5
—— Life and Letters, by Spedding 5
—— Works............................... 6
Bain on the Emotions and Will............ 9
—— on the Senses and Intellect............ 9
—— on the Study of Character 9
Ball's Alpine Guide 22
Barnard's Drawing from Nature........... 16
Bayldon's Rents and Tillages.............. 18
Beaten Tracks 22
Becker's Charicles and Gallus 23
Beethoven's Letters....................... 4
Benfey's Sanskrit Dictionary 8
Berry's Journals and Correspondence 4
Billiard Book (The) 26
Black's Treatise on Brewing 28
Blackley and Friedlander's German and English Dictionary 8
Blaine's Rural Sports 25
—— Veterinary Art...................... 26
Blight's Week at the Land's End 23
Booth's Epigrams.......................... 9
Bourne on Screw Propeller 17
Bourne's Catechism of the Steam Engine.. 17
—— Handbook of Steam Engine...... 17
—— Treatise on the Steam Engine ... 17
Bowdler's Family Shakespeare 25
Boyd's Manual for Naval Cadets........... 27
Bramley-Moore's Six Sisters of the Valleys 23
Brande's Dictionary of Science, Literature, and Art.................................... 13
Bray's (C.) Education of the Feelings 10
—— Philosophy of Necessity...... 10
—— on Force.......................... 10
Brinton on Food and Digestion............. 27
Bristow's Glossary of Mineralogy 11
Brodie's (Sir C. B.) Works.................. 15
—— Constitutional History............ 2
Browne's Exposition 39 Articles........... 18
Buckle's History of Civilization 2
Bull's Hints to Mothers.................... 28
—— Maternal Management of Children. 28
Bunsen's (Baron) Ancient Egypt 3

Bunsen's (Baron) God in History 3
—————— Memoirs 4
Bunsen (E. De) on Apocrypha............. 20
—————'s Keys of St. Peter........... 20
Burke's Vicissitudes of Families 5
Burton's Christian Church 3

Cabinet Lawyer 28
Calvert's Wife's Manual 21
Cates's Biographical Dictionary 4
Cats' and Farlie's Moral Emblems........ 16
Chorale Book for England 16
Christian Schools and Scholars 10
Clough's Lives from Plutarch.............. 2
Colenso (Bishop) on Pentateuch and Book of Joshua 19
Collins's Horse-Trainer's Guide 26
Commonplace Philosopher in Town and Country 8
Conington's Chemical Analysis............ 14
———— Translation of Virgil's Æneid 25
Contanseau's Pocket French and English Dictionary 8
———— Practical ditto 8
Conybeare and Howson's Life and Epistles of St. Paul 18
Cook on the Acts.......................... 18
Copland's Dictionary of Practical Medicine 15
Coolthart's Decimal Interest Tables...... 28
Cox's Manual of Mythology................ 24
—— Tales of the Great Persian War 2
—— Tales from Greek Mythology........ 24
—— Tales of the Gods and Heroes 24
—— Tales of Thebes and Argos 24
Cresy's Encyclopædia of Civil Engineering 17
Critical Essays of a Country Parson 8
Crowe's History of France 2
Crump on Banking, Currency, & Exchanges 27

Dart's Iliad of Homer...................... 25
D'Aubigne's History of the Reformation in the time of Calvin...................... 2
Davidson's Introduction to New Testament 19
Dayman's Dante's Divina Commedia 25
Dead Shot (The), by Marksman 26
De Burgh's Maritime International Law.. 27
De la Rive's Treatise on Electricity 11
De Morgan on Matter and Spirit 9
De Tocqueville's Democracy in America.. 2
Disraeli's Speeches on Parliamentary Reform 6
Dobson on the Ox 27
Dove on Storms 10
Dyer's City of Rome 2

Eastlake's Hints on Household Taste	17
Edwards' Shipmaster's Guide	27
Elements of Botany	13
Ellicott's Commentary on Ephesians	19
——— Lectures on Life of Christ	19
——— Commentary on Galatians	19
————————————— Pastoral Epist.	19
————————————— Philippians, &c.	19
————————————— Thessalonians	19
Engel's Introduction to National Music	15
Essays and Reviews	20
——— on Religion and Literature, edited by Manning, First and Second Series	20
Ewald's History of Israel	19
Fairbairn on Iron Shipbuilding	17
Fairbairn's Application of Cast and Wrought Iron to Building	17
————————— Information for Engineers	17
————————— Treatise on Mills & Millwork	17
Farrar's Chapters on Language	7
Felkin on Hosiery and Lace Manufactures	17
Ffoulkes's Christendom's Divisions	20
Fliedner's (Pastor) Life	5
Francis's Fishing Book	26
——— (Sir P.) Memoir and Journal	4
Friends in Council	9
Froude's History of England	1
——— Short Studies on Great Subjects	8
Ganot's Elementary Physics	11
Gilbert and Churchill's Dolomite Mountains	22
Gill's Papal Drama	3
Gilly's Shipwrecks of the Navy	22
Goodeve's Elements of Mechanism	17
Gorle's Questions on Browne's Exposition of the 39 Articles	18
Grant's Ethics of Aristotle	5
Graver Thoughts of a Country Parson, the Second Series	8
Gray's Anatomy	14
Greene's Corals and Sea Jellies	12
——— Sponges and Animalculæ	12
Grove on Correlation of Physical Forces	11
Gwilt's Encyclopædia of Architecture	16
Handbook of Angling, by Ephemera	26
Hare on Election of Representatives	6
Harley and Brown's Histological Demonstrations	15
Hartwig's Harmonies of Nature	12
——— Polar World	12
——— Sea and its Living Wonders	12
——— Tropical World	12
Haughton's Manual of Geology	11
Hawker's Instructions to Young Sportsmen	26
Hearn's Plutology	1
——— on English Government	1
Helps's Spanish Conquest in America	2
Henderson's Folk-Lore of the Northern Counties	10
Herschel's Essays from the Edinburgh and Quarterly Reviews	13
——— Outlines of Astronomy	10
Hewitt on Diseases of Women	14
Hodgson's Time and Space	9
Holmes's System of Surgery	14
Hooker and Walker-Arnott's British Flora	13
Hopkins's Hawaii	11
Horne's Introduction to the Scriptures	19
——— Compendium of ditto	19

Horsley's Manual of Poisons	15
Hoskyns's Occasional Essays	9
How we Spent the Summer	22
Howard's Gymnastic Exercises	15
Howitt's Australian Discovery	22
——— Rural Life of England	23
——— Visits to Remarkable Places	23
Hudson's Executor's Guide	26
Hughes's (W.) Manual of Geography	10
Hullah's Collection of Sacred Music	16
——— Lectures on Modern Music	15
——— Transition Musical Lectures	15
Humphreys' Sentiments of Shakspeare	16
Hutton's Studies in Parliament	8
Ingelow's Poems	25
——— Story of Doom	25
Jameson's Legends of the Saints and Martyrs	16
——— Legends of the Madonna	16
——— Legends of the Monastic Orders	16
Jameson and Eastlake's History of Our Lord	16
Jenner's Holy Child	25
Johnston's Gazetteer, or Geographical Dictionary	10
Kalisch's Commentary on the Bible	7
——— Hebrew Grammar	7
Keith on Fulfilment of Prophecy	18
——— Destiny of the World	18
Keller's Lake Dwellings of Switzerland	12
Kesteven's Domestic Medicine	15
Kirby and Spence's Entomology	12
Knight's Arch of Titus	23
Lady's Tour Round Monte Rosa	22
Landon's (L. E. L.) Poetical Works	25
Latham's English Dictionary	7
——— River Plate	10
Lawrence on Rocks	11
Lecky's History of Rationalism	2
Leisure Hours in Town	8
Lessons of Middle Age	8
Lewes' History of Philosophy	3
Letters of Distinguished Musicians	4
Liddell and Scott's Greek-English Lexicon	7
——— Abridged ditto	7
Life of Man Symbolised	16
Lindley and Moore's Treasury of Botany	13
Longman's Lectures on the History of England	2
Loudon's Agriculture	13
——— Cottage, Farm, Villa Architecture	13
——— Gardening	13
——— Plants	13
——— Trees and Shrubs	13
Lowndes's Engineer's Handbook	17
Lyra Domestica	21
——— Eucharistica	21
——— Germanica	16, 21
——— Messianica	21
——— Mystica	21
——— Sacra	21
Macaulay's (Lord) Essays	3
——— History of England	1
——— Lays of Ancient Rome	24
——— Miscellaneous Writings	8
——— Speeches	6

NEW WORKS PUBLISHED BY LONGMANS AND CO.

MACAULAY's (Lord) Works 1
MACFARREN's Lectures on Harmony 15
MACLEOD's Elements of Political Economy 6
—————— Dictionary of Political Economy 6
—————— Elements of Banking 27
—————— Theory and Practice of Banking 27
McCULLOCH's Dictionary of Commerce 27
—————— Geographical Dictionary 10
MAGUIRE's Irish in America 23
—————— Life of Father Mathew 4
—————— Rome and its Rulers 4
MALLESON's French in India 3
MANNING on Holy Ghost 20
—————— 's England and Christendom 20
MARSHALL's Physiology 14
MARSMAN's Life of Havelock 5
—————— History of India 3
MARTINEAU's Endeavours after the Christian Life 21
MASSEY's History of England 2
—————— (G.) on Shakspeare's Sonnets ... 25
MASSINGBERD's History of the Reformation.. 4
MAUNDER's Biographical Treasury 5
—————— Geographical Treasury 11
—————— Historical Treasury 3
—————— Scientific and Literary Treasury 13
—————— Treasury of Knowledge 28
—————— Treasury of Natural History .. 13
MAURY's Physical Geography 10
MAY's Constitutional History of England .. 2
MELVILLE's Digby Grand 24
—————— General Bounce 24
—————— Gladiators 24
—————— Good for Nothing 24
—————— Holmby House 24
—————— Interpreter 24
—————— Kate Coventry 24
—————— Queen's Maries 24
MENDELSSOHN's Letters 4
MERIVALE's (H.) Historical Studies 2
—————— (C.) Fall of the Roman Republic 3
—————— Romans under the Empire 3
MILES on Horse's Foot and Horseshoeing... 26
—————— on Horses' Teeth and Stables 26
MILL on Liberty 6
—————— on Representative Government 6
—————— on Utilitarianism 6
MILL's Dissertations and Discussions 6
—————— Political Economy 6
—————— System of Logic 6
—————— Hamilton's Philosophy 6
—————— St. Andrews' Inaugural Address .. 6
MILLER's Elements of Chemistry 14
MITCHELL's Manual of Assaying 18
MONSELL's Beatitudes 21
—————— His Presence—not his Memory... 21
—————— 'Spiritual Songs' 21
MONTGOMERY on Pregnancy 14
MOORE's Irish Melodies 24
—————— Lalla Rookh 24
—————— Poetical Works 24
—————— (Dr. G.) First Man 12
MORELL's Elements of Psychology 9
—————— Mental Philosophy 9
MOSHEIM's Ecclesiastical History 21
MOZART's Letters 4
MÜLLER's (MAX) Chips from a German Workshop 9
—————— Lectures on the Science of Language 7
—————— (K. O.) Literature of Ancient Greece 2
MURCHISON on Continued Fevers 14
MURE's Language and Literature of Greece 2

New Testament, Illustrated with Wood Engravings from the Old Masters 16
NEWMAN's History of his Religious Opinions 4

NICHOLAS's Pedigree of the English People 9
NICHOLS' Handbook to the British Museum 28
NIGHTINGALE's Notes on Hospitals 28
NILSSON's Scandinavia 12

ODLING's Animal Chemistry 14
—————— Course of Practical Chemistry.... 14
—————— Manual of Chemistry 14
Original Designs for Wood Carving 17
OWEN's Lectures on the Invertebrate Animals 12
—————— Comparative Anatomy and Physiology of Vertebrate Animals 12
OXENHAM on Atonement 20

PACK's Guide to the Pyrenees 22
PAGET's Lectures on Surgical Pathology ... 14
PEREIRA's Manual of Materia Medica 22
PERKINS's Tuscan Sculptors 15
PHILLIPS's Guide to Geology 17
Pictures in Tyrol 22
PIESSE's Art of Perfumery 18
—————— Chemical, Natural, and Physical Magic 18
PIKE's English and their Origin 9
PITT on Brewing 28
Playtime with the Poets 25
PRATT's Law of Building Societies 28
PRESCOTT's Scripture Difficulties 19
PROCTOR's Saturn 10
—————— Handbook of the Stars 10
PYCROFT's Course of English Reading...... 7
—————— Cricket Field 26

RAIKES's Englishman in India 23
READE's Poetical Works 25
Recreations of a Country Parson 8
REILY's Map of Mont Blanc 22
RIVERS's Rose Amateur's Guide 13
ROGERS's Correspondence of Greyson 9
—————— Eclipse of Faith 9
—————— Defence of ditto 9
—————— Essays from the Edinburgh Review 9
—————— Reason and Faith 9
ROGET's Thesaurus of English Words and Phrases 7
RONALDS's Fly-Fisher's Entomology 26
ROWTON's Debater 7
RUDD's Aristophanes 25
RUSSELL on Government and Constitution.. 1

SANDARS's Justinian's Institutes 5
SCHUBERT's Life, translated by COLERIDGE.. 5
SCOTT's Lectures on the Fine Arts 15
SEEBOHM's Oxford Reformers of 1498 ...... *
SEWELL's After Life 23
—————— Amy Herbert 23
—————— Cleve Hall 23
—————— Earl's Daughter 23
—————— Examination for Confirmation ... 20
—————— Experience of Life 23
—————— Gertrude 23
—————— Glimpse of the World 23
—————— History of the Early Church... 3
—————— Ivors 23
—————— Journal of a Home Life 13
—————— Katharine Ashton 23
—————— Laneton Parsonage 23
—————— Margaret Percival 23
—————— Passing Thoughts on Religion... 20
—————— Preparation for Communion 20
—————— Principles of Education 20

Sewell's Readings for Confirmation	20
——— Readings for Lent	20
——— Tales and Stories	23
——— Ursula	23
Shaw's Work on Wine	28
Shepherd's Iceland	22
Shipley's Church and the World	19
——— Tracts for the Day	20
Short Whist	28
Short's Church History	3
Smith's (Southwood) Philosophy of Health	28
——— (J.) Paul's Voyage and Shipwreck	18
——— (G.) King David	19
——— Wesleyan Methodism	4
——— (Sydney) Miscellaneous Works	8
——— Moral Philosophy	8
——— Wit and Wisdom	9
Smith on Cavalry Drill and Manœuvres	26
Southey's (Doctor)	7
——— Poetical Works	24
Springdale Abbey	23
Stanley's History of British Birds	12
Stebbing's Analysis of Mill's Logic	6
Stephen's Essays in Ecclesiastical Biography	5
——— Lectures on History of France	2
Stirling's Secret of Hegel	9
Stonehenge on the Dog	26
——— on the Greyhound	27
Sunday Afternoons at the Parish Church of a Scottish University City (Aberdeen)	8
Taylor's (Jeremy) Works, edited by Eden	21
——— (E.) Selections from some Contemporary Poets	25
Tennent's Ceylon	13
——— Wild Elephant	13
Thirlwall's History of Greece	2
Thomson's (Archbishop) Laws of Thought	6
——— (A. T.) Conspectus	15
Times's Curiosities of London	23
Todd (A.) on Parliamentary Government	1
Todd's Cyclopædia of Anatomy and Physiology	14
——— and Bowman's Anatomy and Physiology of Man	15
Trollope's Barchester Towers	23
——— Warden	23
Twiss's Law of Nations	27

Tyndall's Lectures on Heat	11
——————— Sound	11
——— Memoir of Faraday	5
Ure's Dictionary of Arts, Manufactures, and Mines	17
Van Der Hoeven's Handbook of Zoology	11
Vaughan's (R.) Revolutions in English History	1
——— Way to Rest	10
Walker on the Rifle	26
Ward's Workmen and Wages	6
Watson's Principles and Practice of Physic	14
Watts's Dictionary of Chemistry	13
Webb's Objects for Common Telescopes	10
Webster & Wilkinson's Greek Testament	19
Weld's Florence	22
Wellington's Life, by the Rev G. R. Gleig	4
Wells on Dew	11
Wendt's Papers on Maritime Law	27
West on Children's Diseases	14
Whately's English Synonymes	5
——— Logic	5
——— Rhetoric	5
——— Life and Correspondence	4
Whately on the Truth of Christianity	21
——— Religious Worship	21
Whist, what to lead, by Cam.	28
White and Riddle's Latin-English Dictionaries	7
Winslow on Light	11
Wood's Bible Animals	12
——— Homes without Hands	12
Wright's Homer's Iliad	25
Yonge's English-Greek Lexicon	7
——— Abridged ditto	7
——— Horace	25
Young's Nautical Dictionary	27
Youatt on the Dog	26
——— on the Horse	26

www.ingramcontent.com/pod-product-compliance
Lightning Source LLC
Chambersburg PA
CBHW020119170426
43199CB00009B/569